you lost
him at hello

you lost
him at hello

From Dating to "I Do"–
Secret Strategies from One of
America's Top Dating Coaches

Jess McCann

Health Communications, Inc.
Deerfield Beach, Florida

www.hcibooks.com

Library of Congress Cataloging-in-Publication Data

McCann, Jess.
  You lost him at hello : from dating to "I do"—secret strategies from one of America's top dating coaches / Jess McCann.
      pages cm
  Revised and expanded version of the author's You lost him at hello : a saleswoman's secrets to closing the deal with any guy you want, published in 2008.
  Includes index.
  ISBN-13: 978-0-7573-1743-9 (pbk.)
  ISBN-10: 0-7573-1743-X (pbk.)
  ISBN-13: (invalid) 978-0-7573-1744-6 (e-book)
  ISBN-10: (invalid) 0-7573-1744-8 (e-book)   1. Women--Psychology   2. Mate selection.
  3. Dating (Social customs)   I. Title.
    HQ1206.M3643 2013
    306.73--dc23

                                                                    2012045981

Publisher: Health Communications, Inc.
3201 S.W. 15th Street
Deerfield Beach, FL 33442-8190

                                                                    R-08-08

Cover design and cover photography by Jess McCann
Back cover photo by L. H. Lindberg Photography
Interior design and formatting by Lawna Patterson Oldfield

Acknowledgments

To all the agents at Jean V. Naggar Literary Agency, especially Jessica Regel, thank you for all your hard work and support with this project.

To the HCI family, thank you for giving me the opportunity to revise this book. You have all gone above and beyond in supporting me and my quest to help women. A special thank-you to Peter Vegso and Allison Janse for making this revised edition possible.

Contents

ix | **Introduction**

1 | CHAPTER ONE **It's Not Him, It's You!**
The Common Denominator
Then Everything Changed
The Secret to My Dating Success

17 | CHAPTER TWO **A Winning Strategy**
The Truth About Sales
Emotions vs. Logic
Are You Playing Games?

35 | CHAPTER THREE **The Product: You**
Know Your Product
Love Your Product
Packaging Your Product
Attracting Attention To Your Product

63 | CHAPTER FOUR **Finding Him**
Prospecting
The SEE Factor

Icebreakers
Prejudging
Filling the Funnel

97 | CHAPTER FIVE **Getting Him Interested**
Recognizing Buying Signs
The KISS Principle
End at the Height of Impulse
Indifference
The Mirror Theory
The Jones Effect

155 | CHAPTER SIX **Keeping Him Interested**
Hold Back Your Bullets
Don't Cut to the Close
Don't Sweeten the Deal

185 | CHAPTER SEVEN **Closing the Deal**
Never Assume
Fear of Loss
Sense of Urgency
The Silent No
Buyer's Remorse

229 | CHAPTER EIGHT **Maintaining the Right Mentality**
Losing Him at Hello
Don't Drink and Date
The Waiting Game
No Means Next
Practicing in Gamelike Conditions

Introduction

Like most women out there, I used to struggle with dating. Let's face it, at some point, we've all been dumped, stood up, cheated on, or left stranded in limbo. Many of us have failed to take our relationships beyond a casual hookup. And get a guy to commit? Forget about it. You may as well be asking them to cut off their right leg.

Like many of you, I blamed men for all my dating problems. If only he had a better past, a better mother, or a better ex-girlfriend, I would not still be single. But after so many "It's not you, it's me" speeches, I began to wonder. Maybe the guy wasn't at fault. Maybe there was a reason I was hearing the same excuses over and over. Maybe it really was me.

Accepting this revelation was not the end of my problems, unfortunately. In many ways it was only the beginning. Anytime my texts went unanswered, or a first date didn't result in a second, I beat myself up for days. What in the world was my problem? Why didn't men like me? What was it I was doing wrong?

Then, just when all hope seemed lost, a miracle occurred and everything changed. Guys began not only taking notice of me, they started asking me out. My dates turned into relationships, and boys turned into boyfriends. The once pitiful girl who could not give her phone number away was gone, and in true fairy-tale fashion, I met and married the love of my life.

This surprising turnaround would have some claiming divine intervention. For a while, I myself was in disbelief. But it wasn't a higher power that had changed the course of my relationship destiny. It was that I had unknowingly stumbled upon a formula for dating success.

In the past, I use to agonize over every move I made. How should I act? What should I say? When should I call him? Am I too available, or not available enough? These, and many other questions, danced in my head, making me dizzy and knocking me off course. Once I discovered this timeless strategy, however, all those questions were answered. I confidently took hold of my romantic affairs, fully trusting that what I had learned would lead me to love and happiness.

And it did.

I wrote this book because now I want to make your days of rejection a thing of the past. If you have struggled to get men interested in you, or stressed to keep them that way, I can help. Over the last several years I have studied and perfected a strategy to guide women through the dating process and deliver them safely on the other side. The techniques in this book will not only help you date smarter and find love faster, they will protect you from making common mistakes that could sabotage your chances for a solid relationship. Where did I find this insightful strategy? In the least likely place you would ever think to look.

I'm not a psychologist like most relationship experts. At heart, I'm an entrepreneur. Before I became a dating coach, I owned my own company where I hired and trained salespeople. Every day I taught the fundamentals of relationship building to my staff. I coached them on how to pique someone's interest, how to build a strong rapport, and how to close them on a commitment.

This is where the strategy was hiding, just waiting to be discovered.

For years I believed that I was somehow not good enough to hold a guy's interest. I thought if I were just a little prettier, or a little smarter, everything would be different. After learning the ins and outs of smart, strategic selling, however, it dawned on me that it was not who I was but what I was doing that kept me single and lonely. Once I applied my relationship-building skills to my actual relationships, my nonexistent love life finally came alive. Now yours can too.

This book will give you the strategies you need to get the guy you want.

You too can learn, just as I did, how to apply the tricks of the trade to selling your most important product: *you*. Gone are the days of waiting and wondering what to do next. Never again will you second-guess yourself when it comes to your relationships. I'm going to teach you how to find a guy, meet him, get him interested, and keep him that way. Yes, it is all within your control. You are about to learn a proven strategy that will help you take any guy from hello to "I do."

CHAPTER ONE

it's not him,
it's you!

The Common Denominator

"I can't believe I fell for another jerk!"

I was sitting in a café in Georgetown having breakfast with my best friend, Adison. On that particular morning she had dragged me out of bed to talk about her most recent relationship, which, like many before, was headed downhill fast. Before I could even order a cup of coffee, she declared that her latest would-be boyfriend, Gavin, was the offspring of a female canine and then proceeded to give me the play-by-play of their relationship.

"He never calls when he says he will. He acts like he likes me one minute, but then I don't hear from him for days. I am just so fed up with men and their games!"

I listened, as good friends do, as Adison vented her frustrations. She rambled on about Gavin's commitment phobia, how his hot and cold behavior drove her up the wall, and how the next time she saw him, she was going to give him a piece of her mind. But somewhere between the words *jerk* and *player*, I realized that this most recent relationship disaster sounded a lot like her last one. In fact, when I thought about it, it seemed like getting dumped was becoming a pattern for her.

As Adison was about to call this guy a dog for the tenth time, I suddenly realized something: maybe it wasn't such a coincidence that all the guys she dated turned out to be jerks. Maybe there was an actual reason for it. It did seem a little odd that every guy she liked drove her crazy and eventually ended up missing in action, especially since they were all so different. Yet somehow she kept getting the same result. Then, like a ton of bricks, it finally hit me. I knew what was happening. There was only one common denominator in all of Adison's relationships, and it wasn't the men.

"Adison," I said. "Do you ever think maybe it's not him, it's you?"

Adison's jaw dropped. As soon as the words left my mouth, I cringed and waited for her reaction. I was supposed to be her friend. I was supposed to be on her side. I was supposed to call this guy a selfish bastard, not bruise her already damaged ego. In fact, I was just about to recant my statement when she said, "Really? You think I'm making him act this way?"

Up until that moment I truly believed that Adison and I had just been picking the wrong guys. Whenever our relationships got rocky, we would blame the guy for being insensitive, unavailable, or just plain shady. We truly believed that most men were frogs, and we were just going to have to kiss a lot of them to find our prince. But now I had seen the light. Men weren't the cause of all our headaches—we were. If a guy didn't act exactly the way we wanted him to, we would freak out, overreact, and drive him away.

Take Adison's new relationship, for example. This guy, Gavin, did like her. There was definitely a mutual attraction when they began dating. However, Adison started assuming that they were in a relationship after only a couple of weeks, whereas Gavin was still simply getting to know her. She switched into full girlfriend mode before she and Gavin had agreed to be exclusive. So when she started coming on strong, calling a lot, and making all-weekend plans with him, he started to back off.

I was no angel either. I had been just as guilty of overestimated expectations. Yet I continually wondered why men who started off interested in me seemed to always stall on taking that final step toward commitment. Hot and cold were the only two temperaments I'd ever seen from a boyfriend. In fact, the guy I was currently dating seemed to only like me on Mondays, Wednesdays, and Fridays.

Adison and I spent the next hour dissecting all of our previous relationships. In almost every instance, we realized the guys we had thought were jerks were really not so bad after all. We just blamed them for the fact that our relationships had gone awry. We had come up with every excuse in the book for why they behaved badly, when really, we just didn't know how to act with someone we liked. It didn't matter that we were smart, attractive girls. The way we behaved completely turned guys off. What an epiphany! I had to laugh at all the crazy mistakes we had made throughout the years. Looking back, I wondered how I could have been so oblivious.

Suddenly, Adison became panic-stricken.

"Oh my God, Jess, do you know what this means?" She shrieked. "I have been dumped three times in the last year, and I am now realizing it's because of something I'm doing. I'm turning guys off. All this time I thought I was just dating the wrong kind of person. It never occurred to me that I might be bad at dating. Now what am I supposed to do?"

Good question. At the time, I didn't have the answer. Adison and I were fresh out of college and just beginning our lives. If the past was any sort of indicator of what our future would bring, I saw us sitting home a lot of nights, sobbing into a pint of Chunky Monkey. How would we turn things around? Who had the answers? All of our friends back then were suffering from their own dating dilemmas, and most of the books at the time only explained the "why" behind a guy's behavior and not what to do about it. The more I thought about it, the more I feared for the worse. If something didn't change, we might be alone for the rest of our lives.

Then Everything Changed

Ten years after that pivotal conversation I was sitting on my couch wondering why my cell phone had suddenly lost service. It was the great snowstorm of 2009, and I was waiting for my boyfriend, Erik, to shovel us out of the driveway so that we could attend a family Christmas party. I had met Erik the year before while out with some friends and became immediately smitten with him. He was all the things I wanted in a man. He was smart, handsome, and apparently quite handy in inclement weather. I was in love, and for the first time in my life, I believed I had found the person I was meant to be with.

That day Erik joked that like me, my phone was probably just allergic to the cold, but I would find out later that he had purposely hijacked my SIM card so that no one would call me and accidentally ruin the upcoming surprise.

We had finally made our way out of the driveway when Erik suddenly realized he had left his wallet inside.

"I'll be right back," he said as he tore off back into the house.

I sat there still confounded as to why I could not make or take any calls. Erik's phone worked just fine, why not mine?

As I sat there pondering, time ticked on. After what felt like an eternity, Erik poked his head out of the house and motioned for me to come in and join the missing wallet search party.

I climbed up the front stairs quickly and flung the door open, ready to tear the house apart one couch cushion at a time. In my hurried state, I nearly knocked over a lit candle on the floor. What was that doing there? I looked up to see many more candles and flowers placed beautifully around the living room, and Erik standing there in the middle of it all. He was smiling at me, and I suddenly realized what was happening. The moment I had always dreamed of was finally here. The man I loved was going to ask me to marry him.

As he took my hand and got down on one knee, Erik promised to love me, support me, and spend every day trying to make me happy. He slipped the most beautiful ring on my finger and asked me to spend the rest of my life with him. I, of course, said yes.

Turns out, the Christmas party we were headed to was not actually a Christmas party at all. It was an engagement party. All of our family and friends were there to congratulate us on our big news. Erik had dismantled my cell phone because the party had been temporarily postponed due to bad weather, and he didn't want to risk someone calling because they assumed he had already popped the question.

When we arrived at the party, Adison ran up to me and hugged me tight.

"The moment I met him, I knew he was the one for you!" she said. "You are so lucky you found each other."

I gave my friend a smile. "Now you know as well as I do, luck was only half of it."

The Girl I Used to Be

The truth was that relying solely on luck had kept me single and in the wrong relationships for many years. In college, I had an on-and-off-again relationship with a guy named Shawn. I really liked him, and when we started dating again my junior year, I thought we were finally on the same page. I asked him to my sorority formal, which happened to fall on my twenty-first birthday. I was very excited that I would be spending such a big night with a guy I really liked. On top of that, all my friends would be there to celebrate. However, two days before my birthday, he called to tell me he couldn't go with me anymore. The girl he said he "really liked" had just asked him to go to her formal on the same night. I was devastated. I felt rejected. I never wanted to see him again. Unfortunately, he was my next door neighbor.

Another time I fell hard for a Sigma Chi who lived upstairs from me. He would come over all the time and we'd eat, watch TV, and make out. We never defined our relationship, but since we hung out so much, I figured there was no need. He was my boyfriend, as far as I was concerned. Then one day I overheard a couple of girls on the quad talking about him. I listened in and learned that he had been pining away for one of their cheerleader friends who finally decided to go out with him. The next time I saw him, he was holding hands with C-H-R-I-S-S-Y from the squad.

Then there was Danny. I dated Danny for eleven months. I call that time period the Crash of '99. I was head over heels for him. Funny thing was, at first he chased me. He wanted to take me out and I kept turning him down. He called and pursued relentlessly. Eventually I caved in and went out with him. After seeing him a few times after that, I was hooked. The tables were turned, and now I was the one pining after him while he scheduled me in between rounds of golf. My entire week revolved around Danny. If he wanted to hang out, I dropped everything and ran over. I never knew when I was going to see him again, so I took every chance I got. I stopped making plans with friends because I didn't want to be somewhere that I couldn't leave in case he called. It was a disastrous relationship. I was absolutely powerless, and I didn't know how to regain control. So eventually, after many tears, I finally left Danny. He had a new girlfriend three days after we broke up.

So as you can see, I've had my fair share of sad stories. Even after my "It's not him, it's you" epiphany, I still had a number of boy problems and was nowhere even close to getting married. Realizing that I didn't know how to date was only the beginning. I knew that I had a problem—I just didn't know how to fix it.

Fortunately, shortly after college I stumbled upon the formula for dating success. I figured out how to get men interested, stay in control of the relationship, and secure a commitment. My love life started gaining momentum, and guys who had never noticed me before began asking me out. Many of them were discussing exclusivity after a matter of weeks, and several were even talking about marriage. I couldn't believe the change. I was the same person I had always been, but now I was getting the response I had always wanted. The days of being dumped, stood up, cheated on, or left in limbo were over. I no longer had to settle for the few guys that showed interest in me. If I wanted to meet someone, I had a foolproof approach that allowed me to do just that. And, thankfully, it all paid off the night I first saw my husband.

Without my newfound dating strategy, I would have surely blown it with him. He was exactly the man I had been searching for my whole life, and with that kind of pressure, who knows what sort of *I Love Lucy* shenanigans I would have pulled to get him to like me. But luckily I knew how to approach him, how to show him I was interested without being too eager, and how to keep my crazy self from face-stalking my way right out of the relationship.

So what's my secret? How did I finagle a fairy-tale ending from a series of sob stories? It's all laid out right here in this book. And what exactly is the difference between this book and all the others out there? Simple. This book is not based on opinion or secondhand advice. It will not just help you understand men and why they do the things they do. It will teach you exactly how to gain control of your love life and make you effective in dating, regardless of who you are or what you look like.

Now be prepared. This book presents some rather unorthodox advice. But that's a good thing. How many other dating books have you read that have done absolutely nothing for you? This book is different. It won't be like *The Rules*. It does not contain outdated advice passed down from someone's grandmother. And it's not like *He's Just Not That into You*, because honestly, by the time you're done reading this book, he will be. No longer will you sit around with your girlfriends analyzing text messages and waiting for phone calls. You want to land a boyfriend? You want to get married? Well, you can. I am going to show you how to use proven techniques to get the guy you want.

The Secret to My Dating Success

Many years back, when I had just graduated from college, I was trying to figure out what to do with my life. Flipping through the *Washington Post* one day, I saw an ad for a sales job at a local marketing firm. I had never done sales before, and frankly, the thought conjured up visions of used-car dealers. But time was slipping by, and my funds were dwindling, so I went for an interview. I was immediately sent into the field on a ride-along with an established female sales rep. She was my age, sharp, pretty, and had a phenomenal attitude. As we pulled up to an office park in Bethesda, Maryland, I asked her who we were going to see. She replied, "I have no idea. I never set appointments."

Now I was completely curious. She was going to walk in, unannounced, and try to meet with the business owner? How was she going to do that? I watched her as she walked into the first business cold—without calling first, without a contact name—and within minutes was meeting with the man in charge. I was amazed at how she approached her potential customers with no warning and soon had them eating out of her hand. She closed three customers that day. None of them knew we were coming, but they all signed a contract before we left. She created a relationship out of thin air and made it seem so easy to do. Even the customers that didn't buy that day were laughing and smiling when we left. By the end of the day she had made three hundred dollars in commissions. She was so confident, so in control, so powerful. I was sold. I wanted to learn everything she knew.

After I got the job, I immediately began training. It was all so foreign to me—I felt like a fish out of water. But I was amazed at all that I was learning, and the more I practiced my sales techniques, the more comfortable and natural they became. After a few weeks, I was closing my own deals, and after only a few months, I noticed a big change in my attitude. I felt more confident, more secure, more logical. It wasn't that I had just learned to sell a product. I now knew how to get people interested in what I had to say. I knew the best way to get them to like me. I figured out how to win them over.

Then one night after work, I decided to meet up with a guy I had just started seeing. I liked him, but I didn't know how much he liked me. Prior to working in sales, I was always nervous before I went out with someone new. This time was different. I wasn't worried about what he was going to say or how I would respond. I felt totally at ease and completely sure of myself.

Suddenly it hit me.

All the sales techniques that I had learned were applicable to dating! In fact, dating itself was nothing more than a big, fat sale. Salespeople don't just sell products; first and foremost, they sell themselves. There was no difference between winning over a customer and winning over a man. The same strategy applied. Every time I went on a date, all I was doing was trying to sell myself. However, until I landed my job and learned the art of closing the deal, I'd been doing it all wrong. That evening, armed with my secret strategy, it wasn't long before my date was asking when he could see me again.

Spreading the Word

Once I figured out the secret to successful dating, I shared it with everyone. Soon all my friends were using it to meet men and develop their own relationships. I remained in sales for

the next several years, and even opened my own sales training business, but I quickly discovered that I wanted to teach
what I had learned to as many women as possible. So I left
the industry and opened my own date coaching practice. It
was a risk, but what started with just four clients quickly grew
to more than a hundred. Suddenly, girls that had never been
approached before were being chased down in grocery stores.
Ladies that could not so much as leave a toothbrush at a guy's
apartment were being asked to move in. Women that had given
up all hope of finding that one great guy were finally making
their wedding plans.

Over the last several years I've worked with a bevy of clients. I've worked with men and women, both young and old.
Some are truly unaware that something they are doing or saying is giving off the wrong impression. Others fear being alone
so much that it impairs their good judgment. The rest simply
think they are dating the right way because no one has told
them otherwise.

Regardless of the reason, there are a lot of smart, funny,
beautiful women out there who continually get dumped, not
because of who they are but because of what they do. The
truth is that it doesn't matter how great of a person you are.
You could have a double MBA, play the piano like Alicia Keys,
and have legs like Stacy Keibler. If you say or do the wrong
thing in the beginning stages of dating, you are impacting a
man's perception of you. And his perception (as far as he's
concerned) is reality. If you've ever wondered how a guy

didn't see how fabulous you are, it's because you showed him a variety of negatives that ultimately, in his mind, override your good qualities. If a guy senses that you are desperate, needy, overly emotional, unnecessarily angry, or insecure, he will end his pursuit before really getting to know you. Therefore, it is imperative to learn how to present yourself appropriately so that doesn't happen.

Let's be honest. No one goes to school to learn how to date. There are no classes that teach how to appropriately build a relationship with someone. Most of us are just going off our own instinct, or we are doing what we have learned from our parents or peers. The problem with that is that while parents are well intentioned, they dated in a different era. And while all your friends may be following a certain protocol, how many of them are actually in happy, healthy relationships? When asking for advice, you always have to consider your source.

There has only been one time in my life when I actively studied and participated in the fundamentals of relationship building. If you have ever been in the industry, you know as well as I do that sales *is* the art of creating relationships. It's a craft dedicated to stirring interest in people. It's a process that focuses on how to read them, relate to them, and secure a lasting commitment with them. Doesn't that sound like something that could help you with men? It certainly helped me.

Start Strong, Finish Strong

I know what you must be thinking. There is no way you can sell someone on loving you. And you're right. You can't use this strategy to manipulate someone into loving you. But what you can do is make sure you keep seeing a guy long enough for him to get to know who you really are.

The beginning, when the ground rules are being established, is a critical time in any relationship because it ultimately determines the direction the relationship will take. To finish strong, you have to start strong. It's what most women have missed, and salespeople have learned: a rewarding relationship, just like a sale, begins at hello.

Most women I know say or do something early in the relationship that ruins their chances of ever being taken seriously. Even if the relationship carries on for months, or years, the fact that they didn't handle themselves well in the beginning often dooms the outcome. But now you can learn how to date effectively so that you better your chances of a healthy relationship from the very start. You can master the skills needed to peak interest. You can gain the knowledge needed in order to present yourself in the most flattering light, and you can understand the "dance" that happens when two people begin dating, and you can learn to lead it.

Where You Lose Him

Salespeople know if they lose a deal, it's because *they* did something wrong—no one else! Sure, you will hear some of them complain that the customer was too difficult or the territory was too tough, but a good salesperson can tell very quickly who is a good prospect and who is not. A lousy salesperson continues to waste their time on a customer whose chances of buying are slim to none. Either way, the fact remains: when dating, all success and failure comes from you and how you handle yourself.

You will learn in the following pages that just because someone is initially attracted to you does not guarantee that his interest will be sustained over time. At any point in a relationship, you can lose a guy's interest by either using bad judgment or making a poorly thought-out move. Some women lose men after sex. Some lose men on date three. And some women, whether they know it or not, lose men at hello.

If you aren't having any luck in love, whether your obstacle is attracting men, holding on to them, or getting them to commit, your luck is about to change. If you aren't getting the results that you want, you are doing something wrong. We must find out what that something is and change it. What I am about to teach you isn't rocket science—it's just smart salesmanship. And this book will teach you the tricks of the trade so that you will never lose him again.

CHAPTER TWO

a winning strategy

The Truth About Sales

You may be worried that you are in over your head. You've never had a sales job, and, quite frankly, you don't know if you could sell a loaf of bread to a starving man. The truth is you already use sales in your everyday life. From the moment you wake up and decide what outfit is most likely to impress your boss until later that day when you convince your girlfriends where to eat dinner, you are constantly engaging in sales. Whenever you go on an interview, you are selling yourself to an employer. Whenever you try to get a better deal on a car or a house, meet new people, or make new friends, you are drawing on the same set of skills used in sales. Some people are naturally good at reading people and building relationships while other people really need to work at it.

The good news is you don't have to become a superstar salesperson in order to change your love life. You will see that with these techniques, a little goes a long way.

Don't worry if you are a little intimidated. Everyone is afraid of what they don't know or don't understand. Don't tell yourself that this stuff isn't for you and that you just don't work that way. This strategy isn't for one type of person. It's for everyone. If it feels strange at first, it's only because you are stepping out of your comfort zone, which always takes some getting used to. But the more you learn and practice, the more natural it will feel.

While you're learning these various techniques, you will find the answers to questions you had about previous relationships. Questions like, "Why do guys like it when you play hard to get? Why can't I call him? Why is it when I don't care about a guy he's all over me, but when I do care, it never works out?"

But before we dive in, we need to clarify something. As I said before, there are a lot of misperceptions about sales out there. I have friends that think they know how to "sell" a guy on a relationship but have missed the mark completely. These women are like the telemarketers of dating. They bother men with their constant calling, bad timing, and annoying inability to take no for an answer. They subscribe to old adages like, "persistence ends resistance," and so believe, if they just don't give up, they will wear a guy down.

My friend Steve was dating a cute redhead named Sydney. They met at a charity event and hit it off right away. From the very beginning they spent a lot of time together. After just a week, she was already sleeping at his house. Although Steve really liked Sydney, he wasn't quite sure if he was in love. After three months and much contemplation, he decided he needed some time apart to see how he really felt. One night, he told Sydney he really cared about her, but wasn't sure if he was ready for a serious commitment. Of course, upon hearing this, Sydney was distraught. She did not want to lose Steve and was willing to do whatever was necessary to get him to stay.

"I love you!" she declared. "I haven't said it before, because I was afraid to. But I do, I love you. I know that we belong together. Think of how much we have in common. We need to talk about this. Spending time apart won't solve anything. We can work through this. Just give it another chance. You won't find anyone else that will love you as much I do!"

Sydney spent the next three hours trying to convince Steve they were right for each other, and while Steve felt bad about what she was saying, it didn't really change the way he felt about her. Sydney was trying to sell herself, but she was going about it in exactly the wrong way. Steve told me later that the best thing she could have done was give him space. He felt Sydney was becoming too dependent and wondered if she was really the tough, strong, smart woman he initially fell for. If she had understood good sales techniques, she would have used Mirror Theory (you'll learn about that in Chapter 5). Then when Steve had this talk with her, his feelings may have changed. Instead, she begged and pleaded with him, which made her seem desperate. Sydney left Steve's apartment that night and never saw him again.

You can never convince someone to date you, let alone love you, by telling them how much you need or love them. It would be like trying to sell a car by saying, "Hey, I would really love you to buy this car. You don't know what your commission means to me. I've never felt this way about a customer. No one will appreciate your down payment more than I will. I just really need you to buy it. If you don't, I don't know what I will do." Well, that's a convincing argument if I ever heard one! By saying these things, you may make the guy feel guilty or sorry for you, and once in a while, he may even give in and take you back. But it won't make him want to be with you. And that's the whole trick to dating successfully. It's not about getting guys to do what you want—it's about getting them to want you, period. Then they'll happily give you what you need. You will never convince a man to love you by letting him know how much you love him. That's called begging. And it just doesn't work.

Need another example of bad salesmanship? I've definitely got one.

When I first told my cousin Nicole that I was writing this book, she laughed.

"I've done that before!" she said. "I used to sell advertising for a local paper during college. I've tried using sales to date and it just doesn't work."

Curious, I asked, "What exactly have you tried?"

"Well, take Adam for instance. He's a bartender I met when I was out one night with the girls. I thought he was cute, so I was really persistent in getting his number—just the way you are with sales. He said he was in a relationship at first, but after a few hours of flirting with him, he finally gave me his number. We went out a few times, and I totally fell in love with him. But he was so hesitant to commit. We got into a big argument about it, and he told me not to call him anymore. But, in sales you don't take no for an answer. So I called him. He didn't call me back, so I called him again. Anyway, when I never got a call back, I thought about what I would do if a customer didn't call me back—I would go visit them at their place of business. So I went back to the bar and asked him why he hadn't returned my calls. I tried to tell him he was missing out on a good thing, but he looked at me like I was a complete psycho and told me to lose his number. So you see, sales just doesn't work."

I tried to explain to my cousin that what she was doing wasn't sales—it was stalking. Sales is not simply being persistent until someone gives in to you. My cousin's strategy was to bulldoze over this guy. Just like the previous example, she didn't try to get him to want her; she tried to force him to do what she wanted. There's a big difference. Had Nicole learned how to read a man's Buying Signs (Chapter 5), she may have not wasted so much time on Adam and instead found someone more interested in her.

Okay, last story, and then I promise to move on. Ray met a girl on an Internet dating site. She looked attractive and seemed sweet in her profile, so he asked her to meet him for drinks one night. Well, the girl spent the whole night trying to "sell herself." She told Ray she gave great massages and loved to cook in her underwear. She also told Ray that she was the total package, and he should take her off the market before someone else did. That form of self-promotion is not a part of this strategy. Telling a guy that you're a catch isn't going to convince him that you are one. He's got to see it in time—for himself. Yes, it's your job to make him see it, but telling him outright isn't the way to do it. If this girl had known about the KISS Principle (Chapter 5), she would have realized that what she said had the opposite effect of what she wanted.

This strategy is an art form that takes time to master, but once you do, you will see how it can absolutely change your life. There are very few products that can sell themselves without the help of a salesperson. If you had the most beautiful house on the block in the best location and next to the best school, you still would have trouble selling it without a realtor. You would need someone who could find you potential buyers, show them the house, point out its good features, and negotiate a great deal for you. Without that realtor, your house could sit on the market for months without a bite, and you could ultimately settle for a price less than what you wanted.

You are that house. You can either keep dating your way, hoping that someday the perfect guy will stumble upon your house by happenstance, or you can stop dreaming and realize you need to learn to become your own realtor.

Remember, you can't come across as needy or desperate for a sale, and you can't be pushy or overly aggressive. None of those things will entice a person to buy from you, and in dating, the same rules apply. What you will learn in the following pages will teach you just how to behave so that you walk that fine line of being interested, but not too interested, a balance most women have a hard time finding.

Emotions vs. Logic

Understandably, women often rely on their emotions in order to make decisions about dating. We hate that little anxious feeling in the pit of our stomach, and we won't rest easy until something is done about it. Yes, we know we should probably wait for him to call us, but we really want to talk to him. So we pick up the phone and just shoot him a little text. Unfortunately, going with these gut feelings can be very dangerous. When you are dating someone you really like, it's easy to make emotional, rather than rational, decisions. Your heart overrides your head. Now that you've texted with him, you feel better, but what about him? What kind of message did you send by reaching out first? Even though you made a decision that felt right to you, it may have terrible repercussions.

Take my friend Sarah, for instance. She was head over heels for Brody. They had been seeing each other for only a few weeks but got serious very fast. Sarah knew she was in love and was dying to tell Brody how she felt. All her friends thought it was just too soon to say it, and she should wait for him to say it first. But Sarah didn't care. She said her heart was telling her to do it, and she would explode if she held it in any longer. Against all advice from her friends, she proceeded to tell Brody she loved him. To her surprise, he did not say it back. Their relationship continued for a couple more months after that, but Brody eventually broke up with her. Sarah was devastated. Since the relationship felt so right to her, she could not believe that Brody did not feel the same.

Sarah's emotions had clouded her judgment. Because it felt right to drop the L-bomb, Sarah went ahead and did it. Looking back, she wonders how she could have been so rash. Obviously, Brody liked her, but she scared him off by telling him she loved him too soon. Instead of thinking logically about where she and Brody were in the relationship and acting accordingly, she acted based on how she felt. Sarah thought only about what she wanted. She took Brody out of the equation and decided to put her own feelings first. That is why being honest and up front completely backfired on her. Had she followed the strategy and learned how to appropriately assess their relationship from Brody's standpoint, she would not have made such a blunder, and she and Brody may have had a chance.

One Strike, You're Out

Have you ever gone out with a guy a couple of times, had great chemistry, thought you could really have something with him, and then never heard from him again? Unfortunately, this happens all the time. You are left in dating limbo wondering why he dropped off the face of the earth when everything seemed to be going so well. Well sure—it's theoretically possible that some external complication prevented him from returning your call. Maybe he was suddenly shipped overseas, or he was run over by a Mack truck. Things like that do happen. Just not very often.

It's very likely that you made a mistake. Somewhere in the course of dating, you made an emotional decision that felt right to you but turned him off. Just like Sarah and Brody. She made one bad move and he dumped her. Granted, this was the granddaddy of all bad moves, but sometimes all it takes is something small and seemingly insignificant to cause a bad reaction. You may think it's okay to call or text just this one time, but that one time could be one too many. You need to be extra cognizant of what you are doing with a guy so that you don't ruin your chances. In this game, it takes just one strike and you're out.

I'm sure you can think of tons of examples of when a guy did or said something that completely turned you off. It only took one thing, one word, one look, and you were done. Are you really surprised that men are the same way? In the beginning, dating is a delicate affair that must be handled with your head as much as your heart.

Most women try to validate why they do something they know they shouldn't be doing. My best friend Adison knows she shouldn't call a guy the morning after she sees him, but she always comes up with some excuse to pick up the phone and do it anyway. I've heard everything from "He left his watch here" to "I forgot to thank him for dinner, and I don't want him to think I'm rude."

She's not fooling anyone. The bottom line is she's dying to hear his voice. She wants to talk to him so she finds an excuse to validate her decision. She tries to rationalize why she's doing it, but the real reason is emotionally driven. No matter what logical advice I give her, her emotions won't let her accept it. Her stomach tells her she won't feel better until she makes the call. So instead of listening to logic, she listens to her emotions. Then she's completely blindsided when the guy loses interest.

You have to be honest with yourself in situations like this. Instead of trying to find a reason to call the guy you just saw last night, own up to the fact that you are just craving his company. If you are always honest with yourself regarding your emotions, you are more likely to see the reality of the situation and avoid making the wrong move.

Are You Playing Games?

My client Amanda doesn't play games. She is a smart, beautiful, and successful lobbyist in D.C. who doesn't believe she has to. Whenever she meets a new guy, she makes a point of telling them that she is not a game player. Her approach is to be completely open with her thoughts and feelings, so there is no confusion or miscommunication. Yet, Amanda can't seem to hold on to a man. Guys always tell her that they just aren't ready for a serious relationship. She says it's because most men are intimidated by her, but that is just not the case. One day during our weekly session, she looked at me so frustrated and said, "Is there anyone in this city with the guts to seriously date a smart, successful woman? It's like guys only want to date hot girls with low IQs."

I explained to Amanda that her brains and beauty were certainly not the reason she was still single. I told her that if she was getting the same result with every guy, the problem was with her, not them.

At first Amanda became defensive. She did not want to realize the truth and take the blame. "I just disagree with you. I'm a catch. There's no way it's me."

I tried to clarify my point to Amanda. She was right for the most part. She was young and beautiful. It's not that she wasn't a catch. The problem was that she was doing something that deterred men from wanting a relationship with her. In order to get a different result with men, she would have to change her dating strategy. Being so open and honest with her feelings may have worked, if her feelings were that she was happy with her life and not desperately seeking a husband. But I've been working with Amanda for years, and she'll be the first one to tell you that men have always been her primary focus. She will dump her friends in a heartbeat for a night out with a guy. Whenever she meets someone she likes, she cuts off all ties to the outside world, and the guy becomes her top priority. She falls hard and fast, and wants to spend every minute with whoever she's dating in the hopes it will result in a lasting union.

The problem is that men can sense that she is rearranging her life for them, and in the beginning (and really until you are married), that is not the right move to make. Men like to pursue women, not be chased by them. But by being so honest with her emotions and catering to a guy's every whim, that is exactly what Amanda was doing.

"You don't think guys can sense that you're rearranging your life for them?" I asked. "It seems obvious to me that your overeager nature is what's making men back away from you. I know you want to spend time with someone you like, but dropping everything to go out with him when he calls is too extreme, especially in the beginning. I know it's what you want to do, but it isn't always what's smart."

"But I don't want to play games!" she pouted. "If I meet someone I like and he wants to spend the whole weekend with me, why should I pretend I have other things going on? I just want to do what I feel like and not have to play these dumb games!"

"I know it's not what you want to do, Amanda. But unfortunately, it's what you are going to have to do," I explained.

The most common complaint I hear from women is that they don't want to play games. They are too old to play games, too tired, too mature, too pretty, and too smart. Doing what they feel like seems natural, and dating strategically sounds too orchestrated. What they want is to meet someone, be honest about their feelings, and have someone like them for who they are. It sounds good in theory. But unfortunately, these are usually the same women who daydream about moving in with a guy after one coffee date. The more you want and crave a relationship, the more you will have to stick to a strict dating strategy to avoid having your emotions cloud your judgment and lead you in the wrong direction.

Amanda's problem was that because she was immediately making the guy her number one priority, men perceived her to be needy and lacking a life of her own, even though she was a smart and successful woman. If she continued to do what she felt like doing (and not play any games) she would continue to hear the same response from men. Amanda might never be able to change how she wanted to act with a guy, but she could learn to control herself and make better decisions.

Is that playing a game? Does that mean she's not being who she really is? You can think of it that way if you like. I prefer to think of it as having a strategy to get what you want. Amanda could continue to act on her feelings, but the greatest indicator of future events is the past. And her past was pretty lonely.

It's Not a Game — It's a Strategy

You need a strategy to get anywhere in life. If you wanted to start a business, you would need a business strategy. If you wanted to lose weight, you would have a diet strategy. If you wanted to get your finances in order, buy a new house, land a new job, you would need a strategy! So why is dating any different? You want a man, you need a strategy. You would never say something like, "I want to find a new job but I am not going to think too much about it. I'm sure an opportunity will just come my way when I least expect it." Or "I will go with the flow on this interview and let whatever happens happen." Who does that? Yet this is what most women do when they are dating. They expect love to just happen, like in the movies. A man will see them across a crowded room, be awestruck by their beauty, and court them with flowers, candy, and the occasional love poem. A logical plan just doesn't fit into their romance. Well, this is real life and not a "rom-com." In real life you have to be smart and savvy to get what you want.

Ladies, your patterns are making you succeed or fail with guys. I know you are tired of the games and just want to tell a guy who you are and what you're looking for. Well, after spending a number of years in sales, I completely understand. I got tired, too. Sometimes I became exhausted by the effort I had to put forth daily. But that did not mean I could just sit down with a customer and put my naked intentions on the table and say, "You know, sir, I'm tired of pounding the pavement. I'm tired of meeting with different people and trying to make a sale. I am looking for a good customer who will repeatedly buy from me. I could spend the next hour trying to sell you my product, but I don't want to play games here. I just want to know, are you going to buy from me or what?" Can you imagine how well that would have worked?

I am not asking you to change your morals, values, personality, or sense of humor. I don't want you to change who you are. I just want you to change how you date. That will require a strategy, and that strategy will require discipline—discipline to not always do what you want, but instead, to do what is smart. If you've always been one of those girls who hates playing games, let's be brutally honest for a minute. Girls that say they don't play games either:

❶ Don't know how to play,
❷ Are too lazy to play, or,
❸ Don't have enough discipline or patience to play.

Well, before you go any further in this book, make a decision. Are you going to keep making excuses or are you going to start getting results? You can't do both. You have to pick one. Are you willing to stop getting hung up on the whole "game playing" thing and start accepting that you need a strategy to get the guy you want? You haven't had success so far, so something's got to change. That something is *you*.

Relationship Building

The most important thing that sales ever taught me is that building a relationship takes time. It does not happen overnight. In order to truly win someone over, you have to spend ample time getting to know him before even discussing commitment. This is key for single women looking for a relationship. If you are expecting a man to jump into a relationship with you after three or four dates, you are setting yourself up for disappointment. Although you may like someone, and although you may think he is absolutely perfect for you, you cannot rush the progress of your relationship with him. It will scare him off each and every time, regardless of how interested he seemed or how much he pursued you initially.

Dating is a "get to know you" phase. It is a time to have fun, learn about each other, and decide if you are compatible. All this happens before you enter a commitment, not after. If you are guilty of trying to figure out where you stand with a guy right off the bat, you are going to have to downshift back into first gear. It may not be easy for you because you like to know the status of your relationship after a couple of weeks, but you must accept the fact that dating is like being in limbo. It is a temporary holding place for you and a man to spend time together. Once you are there for a couple of months (yes, I said months!), you can then decide if you both want to ascend to the next level together, or part ways and try again with someone else.

I know I may seem like the bearer of bad news, but setting your expectations correctly is going to help you avoid certain heartbreak. Most of what you will learn in the coming pages will be more about what you can do than what you can't, but some of the techniques may still be hard to employ. I promise, however, that if you are up for the challenge, I will show you how to find a guy, get him interested, and close the deal. It's all in your power. You just have to learn how. The rest of this book will teach you all the secrets of relationship building. Starting with learning the basics of the most important product you will ever sell—*yourself*!

CHAPTER THREE

the product: you

Know Your Product

Before I became a dating coach I had a job in medical sales. Ironically, at the time I landed the job, I had zero medical experience. I didn't know anything about hospitals, let alone the cardiac monitors I was selling. But I was always a firm believer that a good salesperson could sell anything. So even if I didn't know the product that well, I thought I could still get by.

After being at my new job for only a few months, I thought I was ready to take my first big client meeting alone. My boss always accompanied me to big presentations, but this time he had a scheduling conflict and couldn't make it. I told him it was no problem because I could handle the meeting on my own.

When I arrived at the hospital I was excited. If my meeting went well, and the client liked our equipment, I was going to make a huge commission. I started setting up the table as the hospital staff began to trickle in.

I began my demonstration by thanking everyone for attending and started going through my pitch. I felt good. It flowed. People were paying attention and nodding in agreement. The usually stoic director of nursing was actually smiling. The head doctor was, too. I thought I had nailed it. But then something happened that I wasn't prepared for.

The staff started asking questions.

I don't know about you, but before that day, I had never heard of ST Analysis. I didn't know how to answer when the director of nursing questioned if the 12-lead report was derived or diagnostic. And when the CEO wanted to know what bandwidth the telemetry system ran on, I wanted to crawl under one of the hospital beds. Just as foreign as this is sounding to you now, they might as well have been speaking Chinese to me back then.

I lost the deal. I left that hospital wondering how I could have been so unprepared. When I told my boss what happened, I expected him to be furious with me. Instead, he said, "I hope you learned a good lesson today. I know you are great at sales, and I know you are great with people. But those things don't matter if you don't know your product. If you don't know your product, Jess, you'll never survive here."

He was right. I didn't know my product well enough to sell it. I tried to make up answers and skirt around issues. At one point I just agreed with one of the doctors when he said he thought our monitors ran on a 608 frequency. I had no idea what he or I was talking about. And let me tell you, everyone in that room knew it.

It is imperative to know your product in sales. Can you imagine going into a meeting and not knowing how to answer simple questions about the product you are selling? Sadly, it's not that unbelievable. There are many salespeople who try to win deals using 100 percent personality and zero product knowledge. I know because I've tried it. However, not knowing how to answer simple questions about your product will leave your customers confused and frustrated, and eventually drive them into the arms of your competition.

In the dating arena, *you* are your product, and in order to really attract a great guy, you have to know yourself inside and out.

Kayla, who is twenty-nine, has always lacked product knowledge. She hasn't had a long-term relationship since high school. Kayla's biggest problem is that she doesn't really know who she is. She hasn't yet figured out the kind of person that makes her Kayla. She spends ample time perfecting herself on the outside, but no time developing herself on the inside. If you asked her if she was a Democrat or Republican, she would say she's not into politics. If you tried to discuss religion, she would tell you she just loves God. If you asked her what restaurant

she wanted to go to for dinner, she would say she's up for anything you want. She hardly has an opinion about anything. I
remember one date asked her, "What do you think about the
war in Iraq?" To this she replied, "I try not to." Yes, she knew
there was a war going on, but that only proved she hadn't been
living in a closet for the last few years. She had no opinion on
the subject. She thought she was being easygoing by staying
neutral, but instead she came off looking like she wasn't smart
enough to form her own opinion. Men find her boring because
she cannot carry on an interesting conversation. She reminds
me of the princess Eddie Murphy was betrothed to in *Coming to America*. He tried to get to know her by asking her what
she liked, and she kept responding with "Whatever *you* like."
And as we all know, the entire movie is based on him chasing
a sassy go-getter from the Bronx so he wouldn't have to marry
the annoyingly passive princess.

I know it's an unusual concept to grasp. Most people never
stop to think about who they really are. But seriously, how can
you expect someone to get to know you if you don't even know
yourself? You may be able to fake it for a while, but believe me,
you will eventually be found out. No one wants to date a Step-
ford wife, so you better start doing some soul-searching and
figure out what makes you *you*. You should be able to answer
questions like, "What are your goals in life? What motivates
you? Are you passionate about music, politics, or sports? What
makes you happy? What really drives you nuts? What would
you be doing if you could do anything?"

If you can't answer these questions off the top of your head, now is the time to really think about them. Men like happy, positive women that have something interesting to say.

Letting Him In

One of my clients, Cameron, is almost forty and has never been married. She is very attractive and has a great job, yet she doesn't get asked out very often. When she does, she typically goes on two or three dates before the guy completely loses interest. At first I didn't know what to think, but then as I got to know her, I realized that Cameron does not like sharing personal information with her dates. She is afraid to let a man truly get to know her. She is much more comfortable talking about neutral subjects, like traveling, current events, music, and movies. Those are fine topics of conversation and you definitely need to find common ground, but it's imperative that you share information about yourself so that men can get to know you. If you are guarded because you are afraid of getting hurt, you will put up a wall that no man can climb over.

You have to be willing to open up and share personal details about yourself. Likewise you have to be able to ask your date personal questions as well. Sticking to safe subjects becomes boring after two or three dates, and your guy won't feel like he's getting any closer to you. How much info should you share? You don't want to tell your date the good, the bad, and the ugly, but you do want him to know a few key things that make you who you are. Tell him about your family. Tell him about your past relationships (when he asks). Tell him about your passions in life or your funny habits (just leave out the weird ones). The key is to tell him just enough about yourself to keep him interested, but not so much that he should send you a bill afterward for three hours of therapy. We will discuss how to balance the self-talk more in the chapter on the KISS Principle, but make no mistake about it, a man will lose interest if he doesn't feel like he's learning anything about you.

Building Your Brand

If you are one of the many women out there who only likes talking about shopping, celebrity gossip, and your coworkers' love lives, you may have a hard time connecting on your dates. Your girlfriends may be impressed that you know how many times JLo's been married or that you can name the entire Jolie-Pitt clan, but that's not going to show a guy how intelligent and funny you are. With men, you need to have more substance to talk about.

I've never been one of those girls who has tried to learn about sports in order to relate to guys, so I am not going to tell you to go out and research his favorite team in order to impress him. I think forcing yourself to take an interest in something that you don't give a hoot about is pointless. If you are not genuinely interested in a particular topic, you will struggle to understand and retain information about it. However, if you open your mind to exploring new things, you will inevitably discover more interests and have a greater chance of finding a guy who shares them.

As much as you want to be with someone who is well rounded, most guys want to find a girl that is as well. So if you are sitting home most nights, texting your friends, checking Facebook, and playing "Draw Something," how do you expect to "wow" the next guy that comes along? The best products on the market are those that communicate a strong sense of what they are. Companies spend time and money researching how to be the best so consumers will buy their merchandise. You, too, have to build your brand. Spend your free time adding "bells and whistles" to your product. Take up a hobby, read a newspaper, try something you have never done before. Invest some time into really developing yourself into an interesting person. The more cool things you can add to your repertoire, the more impressive you will seem, and the more you will have in common with your dates. Just remember that men won't stay interested *in* you if there is nothing interesting *about* you!

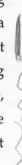

Once You Know Yourself, Be Yourself

There is no better advice from Socrates than "Know thyself." But once you do know yourself, you need to be yourself. You have to be confident and comfortable enough in your own skin so as not to cater to a man. Some girls are afraid to voice their opinions because they don't want to "rock the boat." They are so afraid of the guy not liking them that they would rather stay quiet about things that they don't agree with. But men don't want to date a mindless bimbo who doesn't have her own opinions. If there is one thing worse than a woman who doesn't know herself, it's one who's afraid to be herself.

My father dated a woman who was so afraid to offend him that she never voiced her opinion about anything. She thought if she ever disagreed with what he said, he wouldn't like her. For instance, my father is a die-hard Democrat, and she was a known Republican. Yet whenever they got together and my father started talking politics, she kept her mouth shut. He'd argue a point, and she would just smile and agree with him. Even after a year she was still afraid to speak her mind for fear of offending him. She didn't stick up for her needs in other areas as well. She was never particularly fond of motorcycle riding; in fact, you could almost say she hated it. Yet every weekend she'd smile and get on the back of Dad's bike for a three-hour ride. She figured she was making him happy by always doing the things he wanted to do. But eventually my dad dumped her and told the family that he couldn't stand to be with someone who didn't know how to stand up for her beliefs, even if they were contradictory to his own. He's now engaged to someone who couldn't be more different than he is, and he loves it!

Men aren't offended by differences in opinions. Just because you don't agree with a guy doesn't mean you aren't a likable person. If you don't like something, you can and should say so. You have to figure out if you are compatible, and you can't possibly do that by pretending to be something you know you are not.

Get to know your most important product—*you*. If you don't know your product, you will find yourself constantly struggling to sell yourself. Whether it's expanding your interests or gaining more knowledge for ones you already have, figure out what makes you the person you are. Because if you don't know, you will have a hard time retaining any interested men.

Love Your Product

After the disaster with my first sales meeting, I was sent to New Jersey for follow-up training. All the new sales reps were crammed into a little room and given a chance to ask questions. Most inquiries were regarding standard product knowledge. However, one newbie decided to ask something rather unorthodox. His sales were down, and we all knew that something had been plaguing him since the day he was hired. Whatever it was, he kept to himself, but it was severely impacting his performance. He sat quietly for the entire training, hoping someone else would ask his question for him. When it was apparent that no one was having the same problem, he slowly raised his hand and asked it.

"How do you become successful at selling a product that you don't really like?" he asked sheepishly.

The rest of us sat in silence. How would the teacher answer that? What kind of advice would he give? And what did he think of this rep who basically just announced that he thought our product sucked?

The teacher smiled, walked closer, and put his hand on the rep. "How do you become successful at selling a product you really don't like?" The teacher repeated. "The answer is simple. You can't."

You would think with all the different techniques a salesperson has, liking the product wouldn't be a huge roadblock. Well, I'm here to tell you that if you don't like your product, you haven't hit a roadblock. You've hit a dead end.

In dating, *you* are the product. If you don't like your product and you aren't confident in it, you cannot possibly be successful at selling it. There is a direct correlation between how much you like your product and how much someone else will like it. You will never get anyone to love something you, yourself, do not love.

My friend Ebony doesn't like herself very much. She doesn't eat right or exercise, and she smokes and drinks quite frequently. She complains that she's not in very good shape and that her skin is starting to wrinkle. She is so unhappy with her lifestyle that she beats herself up about it constantly. In short, Ebony does not love herself. When she goes on dates, this poor self-image comes shining through. If a guy is nice to her and actually treats her well, she doesn't like him. Why? Because subconsciously she thinks, *How can this guy possibly like me so much? I'm falling apart. I have nothing good to offer. He must not be very smart. He must be even more worthless than I am.* It's impossible for Ebony to be with someone who treats her better than she treats herself. On the flip side, if she meets a guy who treats her like garbage, she loves him! Why? Because he can see who she really is: someone who does not take care of herself; someone who makes bad choices, is unmotivated, and unhappy. He must be smart. He must be worthy. She chases him and tries to get him to love her. But it doesn't work. You can't get someone to love you until you completely love yourself.

Be Confident in Your Product

Being confident in your product is absolutely essential in sales and in dating. However, if you don't love your product, there is no way to be confident in it. Many women believe that having a man will make them feel better about themselves. They think that getting into a relationship will boost their self-esteem. The problem is that you cannot attract a man when that is your motivation. The smart guys will sense your need for validation and run from you, and anyone else left who is interested will be rejected by you, just like Ebony.

The best thing to do if you are lacking in self-love is to work on yourself before looking for a man. If that means radically changing something about yourself or your lifestyle, do it. If the reason you don't love yourself is because you are engaging in activities that hurt your body, like eating poorly, smoking, drinking, or having casual sex, figure out how to stop. Until you treat yourself well, and feel happiness from within, no man will treat you well either.

If you are simply insecure and worried that you aren't as smart, pretty, or funny as your female friends, men will be able to sense that, too. It's lack of confidence that holds women back and really nothing else. Most of the time men never even notice what it is we are so self-conscious about. They do, however, notice the insecurity we exude because of it.

Back in college I was very insecure about my small chest. I thought I had the body of a fourteen-year-old boy and no guy could possibly like it. I went out with my friends to parties and watched as they all got hit on. I remember standing there, wishing that I had bigger boobs so someone would talk to me. Then one day I told my mother that I wanted to get implants. She looked at me like I was crazy and said, "Honey, it's your head and not your chest that needs fixing."

She was right. It wasn't my flat chest that was keeping me down. It was my insecurity. The more I dwelled on the negative, the more people felt my negativity. The more I convinced myself that no one could find me attractive, the more people agreed. I didn't love my product, and therefore, no one else did either.

Then I realized that I had a choice. I could dwell on something negative about my body, or I could dwell on something positive. I may not have been blessed in the breast department, but I was tall, and I did have nice legs. Anytime I began thinking about my lack of boobage, I immediately switched focus onto my legs. I told myself I had two of the best stems out there. I repeated this over and over. Eventually I began to really love my legs—and the rest of my body. Soon I was walking taller and acting more confidently. Once I started loving myself and believing I was a pretty girl, the guys started noticing me.

Everyone has positives and negatives, but most people tend to focus on what they don't like about themselves instead of what they do like. The truth is that we have many more good attributes than bad. Our mind may frequently focus on our less perfect features, but that is only because we allow it to. If you have two things that you don't like about yourself but ten that you do, don't you think it is better to be grateful and spend time concentrating on the good qualities? Chances are men don't even notice what it is that you don't like. They just notice that you're a Negative Nelly, and believe me, no one wants to date her! If it helps, write down a list of all your good attributes, and whenever your mind drifts to your dark side, think about them instead. Combat your negatives with your positives. They may both be truths about you, but why not spend more time thinking about those that make you feel good about yourself and actually help you attract men?

Turning Around Negatives

For some women it's incredibly hard to be confident, especially when there is something they really dislike about themselves. Maybe no matter how much you work out, you just aren't happy with your body. Or perhaps you've been given some genetic gift you wish you could return. Most people spend hours upon hours thinking and wishing that something they don't like about themselves were different. However, all that wishing doesn't change anything, and if it's something you cannot control or change, you are only adding another negative on top of it. No one likes being around someone who thinks about themselves too much, and that's just what you are doing when you obsess about your lesser qualities.

If what is getting you down is, in fact, something image-related (you hate your nose, your arms, or your butt, for example), try focusing more on improving your insides instead of the outside. Instead of trying to subtract what you don't like about yourself, try adding something that will make you feel better. Having a pretty face or a nice figure may get you noticed, but the physical you is not the only thing that turns a man on. Lots of men think other traits are just as sexy. Can you surf? Cook like Giada? Salsa dance? Guys have even said that seeing a girl drive a stick shift makes her twice as attractive. There are lots of things you can do to up your hot factor and make yourself more confident. You do have to spend a little time developing the skill, but once you get it down, you'll have it forever.

Confidence Is Contagious

When you are out with a guy, be aware that confidence (or the lack thereof) is contagious. During the course of the evening your date may ask you questions that you might not like answering. Maybe he will ask where you live, and your answer is that it's at home with your parents. Maybe he will ask if you work out, and until last week you thought Gold's was the name of a popular jewelry store. You can answer these questions with a scrunched face and a worried look, and your date will immediately know you are unsure of yourself, or you can answer these questions with confidence. Look him in the eye. Don't flinch. Give it to him straight. If he sees you have no problem with yourself, he won't either.

Just remember: you cannot expect anyone to like you more than you like yourself. So if you do not love your product yet, it will not matter how many sales techniques you learn. You will not be able to close the deal. Focus on your strong points. A salesperson never enters a meeting thinking about the chinks in his armor. He thinks of all the positive things about his product. He answers even the toughest questions with confidence. He truly believes he's got the best thing out there! And if you truly believe you are great just as you are, men will agree with you.

Packaging Your Product

A few years back I took on a new client who was having a very hard time attracting men. Even though Adrienne was on four different Internet dating sites, she was not being asked out very often. When she went out with friends, she was hardly ever approached, and when someone did ask for her number, they rarely called. Before I even looked over her online profile, I knew what the problem was. Because she was losing men even before "hello," the issue was image-related. Her pictures online were not flattering, and her appearance in general did not send the right message to available guys. Adrienne was attractive, but she wasn't accentuating her positives. In fact, she was hiding them! She had really great legs but never wore skirts. She had a very pretty face, but didn't wear any makeup. She was very modest by nature and didn't like attention, however, when you are looking for a boyfriend, getting attention is necessary!

I told Adrienne that if she wanted to date and find the man of her dreams, she would have to dress for the part she wanted. The part she wanted, of course, was someone's girlfriend, but she was currently dressing for the role of "soccer mom." She wore tennis shoes or flats every day, along with an old pair of jeans and a loose top. She often threw her mousy brown hair into a ponytail and applied just a dash of mascara before heading out the door.

I convinced Adrienne that we needed to give her a full image makeover. As much as she wanted to hold on to her comfortable and familiar appearance, it was just not helping her meet guys. Her only two choices were to change nothing and nothing would change, or take my advice and spruce up her packaging.

We went to the mall for everything we needed. In full *Pretty*

Woman fashion, we soon had every store clerk helping to select new wardrobe choices. We bought skirts, fitted shirts, and three pairs of high heels. When Adrienne walked into a room, we wanted men to know she was single and looking for attention—something a pair of flip-flops just couldn't do!

We also stopped by a few of the makeup counters, and then ended our spree at a nearby salon. Adrienne had never dyed her hair before, but she confessed she had always wanted to try highlights. With just a little tinfoil and peroxide, her bland brown locks came alive with color, and so did her face! She looked like a new woman; but even better, she felt like one, too.

Clothes do not just make the man. They also make the woman. How you dress communicates a lot about you. First impressions are made from your physical appearance. With that in mind, remember that if you want to get noticed, be taken seriously, and eventually get married, you need to communicate that with the way you dress.

Men are visual. When I say that, I don't mean that they don't understand something unless you paint a picture for them. I mean they are visually turned on or off by what they see. Women are different. Attraction can grow for us. But men know in three seconds if they find someone attractive or not, and, unfortunately, what a woman thinks is attractive is usually very different from what a man thinks is attractive. Women will often overlook things that men cannot get past. It seems shallow, but it's the reality. Sure, there are men who don't place as much importance on appearance, but they are not the majority.

If you are having trouble getting noticed, whether in person or online, you have to take a good, hard look at your image. Is it saying, "I'm single and available" or is it saying, "Don't look at me, I have not showered today"? In Chapter 5 we will talk about "Buying Signs" and how to tell if a man is interested in you. Buying Signs, however, work both ways. Men also need to know that you are interested in having them approach you and ask you out. The very first way you do this is with your appearance. When you dress for the part of an available single woman, you will get noticed. That means wearing the right clothes every day of the week! You may often dress to impress when you are going out on the town, but what if you are just making a stop at the quickie mart? What if you see a cute guy in the checkout line? Or what if you get stuck in an elevator with the office hottie? If you typically leave the house afraid of bumping into someone you know, or roll to work with your hair wet and face bare, then you need to put more effort into your appearance. Remember, you can meet a guy anywhere, so you have to be prepared. I remember a time before I was married when I ran to Kinko's to pick up some business cards, and I didn't do my hair or put on any makeup that day. I was tired, so I threw on a pair of sweats and an old T-shirt. When I got there I was the only one in the store, until an extremely good-looking guy walked in. I wanted to smile at him, but I felt like I wasn't looking my best. So I didn't, and I missed my opportunity to meet him.

I know on Sunday morning it's annoying to shower and dress up just to go out and run errands, but if you are single, it is something that you will have to do. If you only dress your best on Friday nights when you hit the town, you will only have one chance in the entire week to meet anyone. Every day is a potential day to meet your future husband. If you don't look your best the day you meet him, then someone else may end up marrying him!

Do You Need a Makeover?

The best way to figure out if you need to renovate your image is to look at your online profile. If you don't have one, get one. You don't even have to pay to be on some of the sites. Many of them have free trials or allow you to browse without signing up. Dating sites are not only a great way to meet men; they will also do a good job of indicating whether your image needs a little tweaking. If you post a few pictures and are not getting many bites, chances are there is a problem. Most women on sites like Match.com and OKCupid will receive at least ten e-mails the first day they sign up. Traffic will wind down from there, of course, but you should have a number of men wanting to meet you right off the bat. If you don't, that is a strong indicator that your photos and your image need improvement. If you are on a site that makes matches for you, like eHarmony, you should be getting at least three to five e-mails a day for the first week. Anything less points to a problem.

Where Should You Start?

If you know you could use a new look, do not be embarrassed! It's not like they teach What to Wear classes in high school. Chances are you are dressing the way you were taught from your mother or your friends. That's fine, of course, but unless Mom is perusing for a date herself, and all of your friends are successfully meeting men wherever they go, they may not be the best style sources. Start with flipping through magazines to get ideas for new looks. Then head out on your own and ask the people who are absorbed in the fashion industry. When you go to a store, reach out to the salespeople for help. They stand there all day asking people if they need another size. You don't think they would be thrilled if you asked them to recommend some styles for you? Tell them you are looking for "date" clothes—because you are! Not all of them are going to be good at picking out the right look, so ask the women who seem to be sporting an eye-catching style themselves.

The good news is that most appearance issues are fixable. You just have to first admit it needs fixing. If your wardrobe is sending out the wrong signals, change it. Telling yourself you are too tired to put on any makeup or you are too busy to go to the gym will only hurt one person—you. Don't make excuses for a shoddy appearance. If you want to attract a guy, you have to stop doing what's easy and start doing what's smart. If it means getting up an extra half hour before work to straighten your hair, do it! Stop pretending it doesn't matter. It does. No matter how great a product you have, poor packaging can destroy its salability. Men absolutely judge books by their covers, so you need to make yours as spectacular and noticeable as it can be.

The Wrong Look

When my friends and I were in college, we used to go clubbing a lot. Wednesday through Sunday we were out on the town having the time of our lives. We would buy fun clubbing clothes every week so we always had something new to wear. We loved our miniskirts and midriffs. Didn't matter if it was twenty degrees outside; we'd dress like it was the middle of August. We danced with a lot of guys and got a lot of numbers, but we were never taken out to dinner, never called at a decent hour, and never treated with very much respect. We dressed like party girls, and we were treated like party girls. No one took us seriously.

It wasn't until much later in life that I realized that how I was dressing was severely impacting men's perception of me. I was a single girl, but I didn't want to be. I wanted to be someone's girlfriend. I was dressing proactively to get attention and to get noticed. It was working, but not in the right way. I was dressing for the part I had, not the part I wanted.

I have nothing against skimpy attire. If you've got it and want to flaunt it, be my guest. But know the kind of perception you are giving men. You definitely want to be treated with respect, and a bad first impression is hard to recover from. It's a mistake to think all attention is good attention. If a man notices you because your cleavage is staring him in the face, he will be less interested in who you are and more interested in what your cup size is. It's important to package your product appropriately so that you communicate to men that you are available, but not easy.

If you want to attract a man, you have to be willing to dress to do so. It sounds like a fine line to walk, but it's really very simple. Remember that less isn't necessarily more when it comes to clothes. Guys don't have to be able to see your boobs to know you've got them. But also make sure that you are making yourself as attractive as possible. Put effort into your appearance. Men are visual. You want to give them something nice to look at while still leaving something to the imagination!

Attracting Attention to Your Product

When I accepted my job in medical sales, I knew it was going to be challenging, not just because of my lack of product knowledge but also because the company I was working for only had a 7 percent market share. We were the underdog. There were two other industry-leading companies whose monitors were bigger and slightly better. I wondered how I was going to possibly compete with them. How could I attract attention to my product, even though it wasn't as good?

Then I realized that "better" is in the eye of the beholder. Sure, my opponents had a few sleek features that I thought would be nice to have, but my product performed just as well and was equally as reliable as theirs. And in the long run, that's what truly mattered. Although the competition was stiff, I was able to make my quota that first year and even break a new record for the most blood pressure monitors sold by using a simple technique that allowed me to effectively attract attention to my product. Instead of attempting to be better than my superior counterparts, I pitched my product as being different. Being different, in the eyes of many customers, automatically made my monitor more attractive.

There will always be someone out there who is taller, prettier, or thinner than you. So trying to be the most beautiful girl on the planet is a lost cause. I'm not saying you don't need to be the best-looking, most attractive *you* that you can be. I'm just telling you that in order to stand out, you don't have to be more attractive than everyone else in the room. Instead, you can create a style that gets you noticed. Don't try to fit some supermodel mold. Just accentuate the unique person that you are, and you will attract the attention you deserve.

Remember my client Adrienne? After she and I went on our shopping excursion, we put together a few key looks that were sure to get her noticed. She already had a pair of cowboy boots that she often wore under her jeans, but now we decided to pair them with either a cute skirt or a pair of shorts. She pulled her newly dyed locks into a long braid and accessorized with some of the fun jewelry we bought. I sent her out on the town for only two months before she met someone special and started dating him. Then just six months later, she called to tell me she was engaged! She was always a very quality girl, but with her improved new look, it was easy for her to attract the attention she always deserved.

You know yourself very well, and you may easily be able to see what separates you from every girl out there. Unfortunately, men won't know that until they sit down and have a conversation with you, and they can't do that if they don't notice you to begin with. I am not going to lie: in some cities, the competition is fierce. You have to be on your A game when you are single, and that means making sure you always stand out in a crowd.

When I was single I used to wear something different, something eye-catching, every time I went out. Sometimes I wore a hat; sometimes I wore my hair in two braids. I went to my high school reunion in jeans and a funky shirt, while everyone else there was wearing a black dress. When it got warm out, I started wearing shorts with heels instead of a dress—anything I could find to set myself apart from the crowd. I tried on headscarves, jewelry, and funky belts. Sometimes I would dress up if I knew everyone else would be dressing down, or I would dress down when everyone else was dressing up. There was no right or wrong. All that mattered was looking different.

Repeat Your Best Outfits

Whenever Adison goes running, she wears her Yankees cap. She usually stops for coffee when she is done working out, and someone almost always comments on her hat. Knowing this, I told her she should incorporate the hat into her daily wardrobe.

You need a couple of staple outfits that are sure to grab a guy's eye. The great thing about trying to be different is that you not only get noticed because you stand out, you also have a conversation starter. Men love it when you give them a reason to come talk to you. It takes the pressure off of them for coming up with something to say.

I used to have five outfits that were always able to get me noticed, and I wore them a lot. My girlfriends would call and ask me what I was wearing that evening, and I would tell them "outfit number four." It doesn't matter if your friends have seen your favorite blue dress a hundred times, they aren't the ones whose attention you are trying to grab. If you know that certain things in your wardrobe drum up a lot of business, wear them often! Don't buy new clothes that will only make you blend in. Try new styles that are a little unusual, and see what kind of reaction you get. If you notice another female while you are out, ask yourself why you noticed her, and then copy what she is doing. I once noticed a girl running in front of my apartment because she was wearing a hot pink running suit. Now I own one as well.

Keep What Makes You Unique

These days, plastic surgery is on the rise. It seems like everyone wants to fix that little imperfection that has always bothered them. Maybe that bump in your nose annoys you, or you've always dreamed of fuller lips. But unless you have some truly irregular feature that is severely impacting your social life, I recommend embracing the things that make you, *you*. The more you try to change yourself to look perfect, the more you will end up blending in with everyone else. Heidi Montag, anyone?

Cindy Crawford was and still is one the worlds' most popular and beautiful women. However, Cindy did not always see herself that way. Growing up, she was very self-conscious about the mole above her lip and contemplated getting it removed. Her first modeling pictures were actually airbrushed to hide the mole, and many thought she would never make it big with a mark on her face. But they were wrong. That mole separated Cindy from the thousands of girls aspiring to be supermodels. The mole became her trademark and took her to the top. She became a sex symbol that was revered and imitated by girls around the globe. It just proves that different can be sexy. Very, very sexy!

Don't shy away from something that makes you different. Embrace it. My sister is blind as a bat, but instead of getting contacts, she got glasses. They make her stand out and seem very sophisticated and sexy. Fitting in and looking like everyone else is boring. You want to be different—doesn't matter if it's because of some characteristic that isn't normally classified as attractive. Justin Timberlake was once quoted as saying, "I have a big nose, but I rock it!" Usually big noses are not a symbol of sexy, but last time I checked, JT was the one bringing it back. And you can do that too.

CHAPTER FOUR

finding him

Prospecting

By the time I finished my first full year in medical device sales, I had achieved 120 percent of my quota. This shocked a lot of people. My assigned target of $2.1 million in revenue hadn't been met by the previous sales rep for years, and no one thought a young, inexperienced saleswoman was going to do any better. When I attended the national sales meeting, I was congratulated by my coworkers (who all happened to be men). When the commotion finally settled down, I decided to relax by the pool with my good friend Lou. Lou had been a medical sales rep for more than six years. This year, like the last year, he had just missed his quota. As we sat by the pool talking numbers, I wondered how it was that I outsold him by almost a million dollars. Here he was, a seasoned rep that knew the product better and had stronger relationships with his customers. Yet he was beaten by a young rookie that had no prior medical experience. Lou and I talked almost every day, so I knew he was a hard worker. He seemed to get up earlier and work later than I did. And he was always in a hospital or at least driving to one, so I knew he wasn't sitting at home. So how in the world had I closed more deals than he did?

Before I even got the question out of my mouth, Lou was already answering it.

"Prospecting," he said. "I hate it. I don't do it. I may go to hospitals every day, but they are hospitals that have already bought from me, or hospitals where I know people really well. I never go to new hospitals and look for new business. I hate introducing myself to people that I don't know and asking if they need anything. I just want them to call me. I don't like stepping out of my comfort zone."

I thought about what Lou was saying, and it made perfect sense. Unlike him, I prospected every week. I would spend days at a hospital that didn't have my equipment, introducing myself and making new contacts. I was always trying to find new business, whereas he was just maintaining what he already had. That reason alone is why I outsold Lou. Prospecting is a necessary and essential part of success in sales. However, it's also one of the most important factors in dating.

My sister Lisa and I could be twins. We're the same height, weight, and thanks to Feria 205 color treatment, we now have the same hair color. We also have very similar personalities and senses of humor. Years ago we happened to break up with our boyfriends at exactly the same time. Right away I thought, *This is great! We will be single together and keep each other company!* However, Lisa immediately started going on ten times as many dates as I did. She had a date at least twice a week, whereas I was lucky if I had one date a month. What was the reason? She went prospecting. Lisa dedicated two nights a week to looking for potential guys. She would attend happy hours, work functions, and restaurant openings. Not only that, Lisa also made sure to try new places. She hardly ever went to the same place twice, unless she found it to be a good place to fish for men. Meanwhile, I was going out to the same bars and clubs with my friends. Just like Lou, I did what was easy instead of what was smart. My philosophy was, "Let's go where we have fun, and if something comes up, great. If not, that's okay." And that's a fine attitude to have, but it's not conducive to finding a man. Within six months my sister met the guy who would later become her husband, while I was still very single.

If you are ready to have a relationship and would like to get married in the next three to five years, it's time to get serious and put some more effort into prospecting. I hate to tell you this, but fate won't deposit a boyfriend on your doorstep anymore than it would have sold my equipment for me. If I wanted to make quota, I had to get out there and make it happen. I had to meet new people, introduce myself, and show them what I had to offer. If you really want a relationship, you are going to have to do the same thing. I know it's uncomfortable to put yourself out there—believe me, prospecting was not my favorite thing either. But if you want to find The One, you have to accept the fact that you will need to put some time and effort into looking for him.

Lauren, who has been single for five years, hates going out. She would much rather rent movies or cook dinner for her friends. She wants to meet someone and get married, but the problem is, she doesn't really do anything to help her cause. She just complains about never meeting anyone.

One day I said to her, "Lauren, where do you think you are going to meet someone? In your stairwell? You never go out and put yourself in a situation where you could meet anyone. He's not going to come knocking on your door, you know. You have to take matters into your own hands. You have to put yourself in a position to meet people. You need to get out more, and you should definitely put yourself online."

"I just don't think online dating works," she complained. "And I went out all last year and never met anyone. All the guys around here are either workaholics or party boys. I'm not going to find anyone intellectually stimulating in a bar. So why go out at all? I'm happier at home."

"Just because you didn't find anyone last year does not mean you won't find anyone this year. You have to keep going. In sales we have a saying: Every no brings you closer to a yes.

If you always went to the same bars and saw the same people, of course you didn't find anyone. You never went anywhere new, so you never met anyone new. If you really think all the men around here aren't worth your time, then by all means, go ahead and stay home. But please don't complain about it. It won't help you find a guy, and it won't change your situation."

Lauren knew I was right. If she wanted to get married, she would have to start creating opportunities to meet men. Like many women, she was holding on to the old adage that love would strike when she least expected it, and it was seriously hurting her chances.

The idea that we don't have to do anything and the man of our dreams will find us is just not realistic. If that's how you think, you need to put down the Nora Roberts novel and come back to real life. Men and women these days are extremely busy. If you don't put the effort into looking for your future husband, you very well may never find him. I know that is scary to hear, but it's true.

If Lauren wanted to change her luck, she was going to have to change her methods. When I asked her what her schedule for the week was like, she would tell me she was busy with lots of plans, but none of them were prospecting opportunities. She would go to her parent's house for a visit one day, to the movies with a friend another, and then to yoga or book club. She was doing activities that were filling her time, but there was no way she was going to meet anyone with a schedule like that.

Think about your week right now. What are your plans? Are they conducive to prospecting? Or will you be sitting somewhere that will give you very little opportunity to meet someone? If the answer is yes, then you need to modify your agenda.

How to Prospect

The smart way to prospect is to go where the most opportunity is. For instance, there are more guys at the driving range than at the mall. Instead of hanging out at your girlfriend's house where the only guy around is her kid brother, go to sports bars and pool halls. Coffee shops are also a good place to meet men. You have to be creative and think to yourself, *If I were a guy, where would I be?* I have met a couple of very cute boys at my local dog park. The funny part about that is that I don't own a dog. But I would walk there with a girlfriend, and when a guy asked which dog was mine, I would tell him that I was thinking about buying one and was just checking out my options. Guys are more than happy to tell you about how great their pup is, and before you know it, they will be asking for your number.

Prospecting Events

Every weekend there is something going on in your particular city that will bring out the boys. You just have to search for it. Contrary to popular belief, I think meeting guys at bars and clubs is totally possible, because the sole reason they are there in the first place is to meet girls. The mentality that you can't meet a good guy at a bar is just not true (as I will demonstrate later in the book). Guys who are out in the bar scene are sociable, have lots of friends, and are open to making new ones. They wouldn't be there otherwise. Yes, you may have to sort through a few duds, but there are good candidates out there too.

You just don't want to prospect at a bar late night. Any guy who is partying hard into the hours of morning is not as prime for the picking. Stick to happy hours in order to meet the more professional types of men. I never stayed out past nine when I began seriously prospecting, and it always worked well for me. Begin your night right after work, and take yourself home before the drunken crazies come out!

There are certain places and events that you can also bank on for good prospecting. For example, restaurant openings and wine tastings are fantastic opportunities for prospecting. And I remember St. Patrick's Day being a feast for my girlfriends and me. Every man in Washington, D.C., was out and about from ten in the morning until ten at night. Have you ever noticed how many men run marathons? Sign up! If that's too extreme, check out a 5 or 10k in your neighborhood. I bet you find a plethora of healthy, hot guys there.

Get Creative

Besides seeking out guy-friendly places, you can also change up your daily routine. Go to different grocery stores, switch gyms, try a different church. I switched hairdressers and once ended up dating the owner of a very trendy salon. It's not just about going where you think the guys are, although that is definitely a good strategy. It's also about putting yourself in different places at different times. Change up your daily routine and see what happens. I used to go to the same grocery store every Saturday morning, until one day my friend met a guy at Whole Foods. She told me that Monday nights at Whole Foods is a prospecting bonanza! Every guy in our city shops there, and for some reason, they go on Monday nights.

Make sure you don't get stuck in a rut with your daily routine. Don't always go to the same Starbucks. If you belong to a health club, try another location. Get creative about where you look for men. You may find one right in your own backyard.

The Law of Averages

One thing to remember about prospecting is that even the best saleswoman doesn't find new business every day. Sometimes we don't make a breakthrough for weeks, or even months. I can remember prospecting different hospitals all summer without a bite. It seemed like I was never going to find a new customer. But then, all of a sudden, I hit the jackpot and found a hospital that was building a whole new wing. Those three months of prospecting paid off considerably.

The Internet is a great place to increase your law of averages, especially if you are like Lauren and would rather not leave the comfort of your own home. It's one of the best places to prospect because a bar or party can only fit a finite amount of people, whereas online sites are filled with millions of men. Your chances of meeting the right guy are increased exponentially by the use of the Internet. The old stigma of online dating has just about disappeared. If you're still hesitant about joining a dating site, then you can use less specific networking sites. I know many of my clients have met great guys through Facebook and LinkedIn. Being on the site doesn't necessarily mean you are looking for a relationship, so you (and your potential dates) may be a little less squeamish about logging on. Just be smart and careful about meeting people you don't know. Don't put out too much personal information right away, and always tell a friend who you are meeting and where you are going.

Just remember, your future husband doesn't know where you live, so you have to get out there and make your presence known. Sitting at home and doing nothing may be what's easier, but it won't get you what you want. Don't get discouraged if you have been prospecting for months and haven't met anyone. It will take time. You will not find someone you like every time you go out. That is a certainty. But if you keep prospecting you will eventually find him. It's the law of averages— a numbers game. Every no will bring you closer to a yes. And the more times you go out, the better your chances.

The SEE Factor

When I went to the Sundance Film Festival many years ago, my girlfriends and I made it our mission to find single guys. We got dressed in our cutest winter gear and went out every night prepared to party and prospect. One of the girls in the crew, Leah, was attracting far more men than the rest of us. She was getting two and three phone numbers every night, while the rest of us just watched in awe. After our third night there, one of the other girls announced that Leah was a guy magnet! She just had "It"—that unexplainable quality that men love. Even though the rest of us were equally as attractive, guys naturally flocked to her.

But I knew that wasn't it. Leah was doing something that the rest of us weren't. She was doing something so simple, that even as my friends watched her, they still didn't see it. She was using her SEE Factor.

What Is SEE?

Some women would rather jump off a bridge than approach a man. We have been taught to let him come to us. Or, as The Rules would instruct, smile at the room and look like you are having a good time with your friends. Don't make eye contact. Make it seem like you are hard to get, so that you don't seem needy. He needs to come over and get your attention so that you keep the element of "the chase" going, right? Wrong.

Guys need a sign that you are willing and interested to talk. Walking over to a girl and starting a conversation is very scary. Most guys would feel more comfortable addressing Congress. Knowing that, you need to give him an indication that he won't be immediately rejected. In sales we use something called the SEE Factor. We use it when approaching someone for the first time. SEE stands for three things: ❶ smile, ❷ eye contact, and ❸ energy. When I would walk into a customer's office, I would smile, make eye contact, and exude good energy. This puts the other person at ease immediately. Applying the same method to dating is simple. When you see a guy you think you might be interested in, walk by him, smile, look him right in the eye, and let him sense your good energy.

I know—easier said than done, right? The reality is you have most likely never done this before, and it will take several times to get comfortable with it. But in order to get what you want in life, you will eventually have to try new things, so you may as well start now.

I watched Leah when we went out and saw how she used her SEE Factor. The rest of the girls huddled together and didn't make eye contact with anyone. Leah would walk around the room smiling, looking men in the eye and exuding a very positive and friendly energy.

Leah knows how to prospect. She makes twenty trips to the bathroom (the long way around the bar) so that she can continually SEE and be seen. She isn't afraid to make eye contact and smile. That is what makes her a guy magnet. If the other girls had not been isolating themselves and made more of an effort, they would have gotten the same results.

I am not asking you to do much here. Just think of how hard guys have it. They actually have to think of something to say. Then they have to stand there, wait for you to accept them, and engage them in conversation or reject them and send them on their way. You don't have to worry about any of that. You walk by the guy, smile, give him a good "one Mississippi, two Mississippi" eye lock, and keep walking. The energy part of the SEE Factor is your prospecting attitude. You want to exude good energy, which means being confident and positive. Guys don't want to talk to chicks who are in bad moods, having a lousy time, or feeling bad about themselves, and believe me, they can tell.

If you have been going out regularly and wondering why no one has ever approached you, ask yourself what sort of signals you are putting out there. Are you trying to catch someone's eye or are you playing aloof and avoiding eye contact at all cost? If you think just putting yourself in a situation where a guy could potentially spot you is doing enough on your part, think again. Nine times out of ten men will approach a less attractive girl if she seems receptive to talking than one he thinks is prettier but who may possibly shoot him down.

All you need to do is give him the SEE and he'll make the next move. You may have to give it to him two or three times so that he can be sure you really are looking at him, but once he gets the message, he'll soon be asking to refill your cocktail.

If you are prospecting outside, maybe jogging or at the park, I strongly recommend losing the sunglasses. There is no way you can appropriately execute the SEE Factor while wearing them. Besides that, no man will ever approach a woman with sunglasses because they put up a huge wall between you. They have no idea what you are thinking with them on. Are you looking his way? Did you notice him when you walked by? Do you seem like a friendly person? Who knows? You are wearing huge glasses the size of Texas. He can't see your eyes—he's not coming over.

The Fear Factor

I guarantee that a lot of guys would like to approach you, but their fear of rejection keeps their feet planted where they are. There is nothing sexier than a woman who is confident in herself, and looking a man in the eye conveys complete confidence. If you get nervous, just remind yourself that all you are doing is smiling at someone. How is that bad? You may feel fearful at first to practice the SEE Factor because you have spent so much time avoiding eye contact up until now. If you feel anxious when you try it, just put yourself in the guy's shoes. If he smiles at you and you quickly look away, what message do you think he will get from that? Most likely he'll assume that you are not interested, worry that you think he's weird, and suspect that you may press charges if he dares to chat you up. Then he will likely go home feeling depressed and dejected all because you averted your eyes when he looked at you. Think in terms of him and his feelings when you get self-conscious. Take the focus off how you feel and what you fear. It may take some getting used to, but I guarantee, if you begin to make the SEE Factor a way of life, you will bring yourself many opportunities and good fortune.

Icebreakers

When I turned thirty-one I decided I really wanted to meet the right guy and settle down. I had dated a few guys over the years, but hadn't found anyone truly special and spent most of my time concentrating on my career. In January 2008 I made up my mind that I would put some serious effort into prospecting and make finding my future husband a top priority.

I forced myself into some type of social setting two to three nights a week. I also dedicated a few weekend hours during the day for prospecting at various guy-friendly places. It quickly began to pay off as I began meeting men, going on dates, and formulating new relationships.

One night, I walked into a restaurant called the Liberty Tavern with two girlfriends. We sat at a long, high tabletop that stretched across one end of the room to another. On the other side of the table stood three guys, one who I particularly noticed right away. He was tall, cute, and dressed in a suit. The only problem was, he was not standing facing my direction, so giving him the SEE Factor was not an option. I had to get his attention another way.

"Excuse me? Could I borrow your menu?" I asked.

"Absolutely." He smiled as he handed it over.

It wasn't clever, original, or funny. In fact, it was as benign an opening line as you could get. That's okay though. My question served its purpose. Moments later we were engaged in conversation that carried on for hours. As we chatted and got to know each other, a lightbulb went off in my head. I knew I had met someone very special . . . someone I wanted to know better. And even though I wouldn't know why I felt this way for many months to come, I would later come to know that this was the very first conversation I had with my husband.

Most women do not want to make the first move. In fact, most other books will tell you not to make it because you will come off as too aggressive or desperate. The truth is, it is totally fine to approach a man—if you know how to do it. If I had not approached my husband, I may not have ever met him. He told me he noticed me right away when I walked into the bar, but that he was exhausted from the workweek and not in the right frame of mind to approach someone. Once I opened the conversation and smiled at him, however, he happily engaged. How many guys do you think see you while you are out and simply feel the same way?

The problem isn't that talking to a man first may ruin your chances; it's what you are saying to that man that may ruin them. So what exactly can you say when you're making the first move? The trick to starting a conversation is to use an Ice-breaker, a small remark or question that can be directed toward just about anyone—something that seems spur-of-the-moment, unintentional, and casual. When you are the one approaching a man, you want your opening conversation to seem aimless. You don't want the guy to know you have an agenda to meet him.

Forget Playing Hard to Get

Many women still hold the belief that you have to play coy when meeting men. They trust that if a man is truly interested, he will get off his bar stool, cross the room, break up the con-versation you are currently having with your friends, and introduce himself. Well, as much as I hate to debunk anyone's romantic fantasies, if this is one of yours, it's likely to be the reason you have a hard time meeting guys.

When you are out and you see a guy you might like to meet, you no longer have to sit there twiddling your thumbs, pray-ing for him to notice you. You can (and should) start a conver-sation with him. Someone has to do it. Why not you?

Can you imagine if salespeople had the attitude that they were not going to approach customers? They would be out of a job pretty fast. Much like them, you have to go after what you want. It's not being aggressive as long as you use the right method of approach. If you are worried about being rejected, don't be. When you use an Icebreaker, you cannot possibly be rejected. If a guy doesn't continue the conversation after you break the ice, so what? You weren't even hitting on him in the first place. You were just borrowing his menu or asking for the time. Opening with an Icebreaker will keep a guy from sensing your agenda right away. You don't want him to think you are prospecting for a husband, and by using this technique he won't suspect a thing.

The best thing about Icebreakers is that you can use the same one over and over. You don't need to come up with a different one every time you go out. The guys will never know.

Several years ago my friends and I went to Oktoberfest determined to meet new people. We decided that when we saw a guy we wanted to talk to, we would stop him and say, "Hey, don't you go to my gym?" The guy would say no, but he almost always engaged in conversation after that. With the six of us prospecting, we probably asked fifty guys this question. It was fun, and we all got several numbers from doing it. (Remember, dating is a numbers game. The more people you meet, the closer you get to finding someone you like!)

Try and think of some standard Icebreakers so that when you come across a guy you want to meet, you don't struggle to find something to say. It's a good idea to think of Icebreakers ahead of time, otherwise your nerves will get the best of you and you may end up missing your chance. Some Icebreakers that are good to have in your back pocket are:

Do you know if there is a wait for a table?
Can you take a picture of my friends and me?

Do you know what the happy hour specials are?

Aren't we friends on Facebook?

That drink looks good, what is it? (This works well at places like
Starbucks.)

Didn't you go to my high school?

You can use the above Icebreakers at any bar, club, party, or restaurant. If you are someplace like a grocery store, you can follow a guy to the wine or produce section and ask him if he knows how to pick a good pinot or avocado. Usually, this is all it takes for you to open the lines of communication. The guy will take over from there.

Don't worry. It can be the lamest Icebreaker on Earth, and it won't matter. I have a friend who is an aesthetician, and she loves to break the ice by asking men if they have ever been waxed! I'm not kidding. Say anything and he'll continue the conversation from there. Guys love it when women make the first moves in these situations. I know, because I have done it myself. Not once has a guy told me he would rather do the approaching. Remember—you aren't asking him out, you're just being friendly and sociable. There is a big difference.

Be aware of opportunities that you can break into and make contact. Armed with these tactics, you can start talking to any guy you find while prospecting, and who knows, you may also meet your husband this way as well!

Prejudging

Mallory and Megan are best friends and two clients of mine. They had decided to seek out my help when they both turned twenty-nine and began to worry about whether or not they were ever going to get married. Mallory had had a long-term boyfriend in college, but they broke up when they graduated and she has been single ever since. Megan had had a string of short-term relationships in her early twenties, but in the last four years she had gone through a major dry spell. Both girls wanted to find love and get married, but neither of them were meeting anyone of interest. The few men they did find interesting only took them on a few dates before abruptly announcing they weren't looking for anything serious.

Since Mallory and Megan were both having trouble just meeting men in general, I knew that something about their prospecting method was off. They were both attractive girls who went out quite a bit and maintained online profiles, so theoretically they should have been going on a lot of dates. I decided in order to find the root of the problem, I would have to shadow them on a night of prospecting to see what I could see.

It didn't take me long to figure out what the problem was. On the night we went out, the girls hit three restaurant bars in a span of forty minutes. They walked in, took one lap around the bar, and announced to each other, "There is no one good here. Let's try somewhere else." At each place they surveyed the crowd for someone they thought was cute enough to start a conversation with, and quickly assessed that no one was worth their time.

Before I gave the girls my diagnosis, I wanted to check out their online conversations to confirm my suspicions of what was keeping the boys away. When we got back to their apartment and hopped online, the proof was in their profiles. They both had a slew of potential prospects winking and e-mailing them, but both Megan and Mallory only responded to a very select few.

I sat the girls down the next day at lunch to explain what needed to change.

"You'll be happy to know that your problem is 100 percent fixable, ladies," I started. "If you tweak just one thing, you will see improved results overnight."

"Great!" said the girls. "What is the problem? What are we doing wrong?"

"You are prejudging," I said. "You are both doing it, and it's what is preventing you from meeting anyone."

"What do you mean?" Mallory asked. "I don't think we are prejudging."

"Oh no? You walked into three bars last night and walked out within a few minutes because no one had the exact look you wanted. You are judging men on their appearance and nothing else," I said.

Megan started to argue with me. "I don't think that is pre-judging. I think we are just looking for someone we are attracted to. Unfortunately, there just aren't many men out there that are fitting the criteria," she stated.

"Listen, you are judging men on their appearance, from the color of their hair to their style of their shoes. Megan, you didn't want to talk to one guy because he had facial hair. Facial hair that, if you didn't know, can be shaved off! You both are too particular about what you are looking for physically in a man. That is what is keeping you single. If you are only judging a person based on their appearance, then you are only going to be attracted to the top 2 percent of men. That's not a lot of guys to choose from. You may finally find a guy who has everything you want, but you will be eighty years old by then and he won't want you."

"I just know within thirty seconds who I am going to be attracted to," Megan stated. "If the spark is not there at the beginning, it's not ever going to be there. I'm not going to settle for less than what I want!" she cried.

I looked at Mallory, who was still processing the information.

"I guess I see your point," she said. "I know that in the past I have developed attraction for some of my guy friends after getting to know them because they were super smart or funny. I guess what you are telling us is that we have to give more people a chance to see if some of their other qualities override physical attributes we may not be fond of right away?"

"Exactly. You have to put more stock into other characteristics. Humor, intelligence, integrity, and kindheartedness are all very attractive qualities that can really add to a man's appeal.

You aren't able to see these things with the naked eye. You have to get to know someone first, and that means giving men who maybe aren't exactly your type physically a chance to show you how hot they are in other ways," I told them.

Mallory seemed to be coming around. Megan just sat there looking quite unhappy.

What Are You Looking For?

Every girl has a type they like physically. Maybe it's a guy who is over six feet or hair that is dark and wavy. There is nothing wrong with knowing what you like aesthetically, but when you only judge men on their outward appearance, you are superficially looking for a mate and placing more importance on qualities that actually won't matter in the long run.

When I was first visiting hospitals I was told to visit every single one in my territory. My manager told me not to cherry-pick and go to places that had the potential for bigger sales. It was hard though. Smaller hospitals rarely made large purchases because they lacked the budget and didn't have the need. But I listened and still prospected the tiny facilities because I didn't want to prejudge. On my third day I walked into City Hospital in West Virginia, not expecting much in the way of a sale, but surprisingly enough, the director of nursing said they needed sixty new blood pressure monitors! It was the largest sale I made that year, and because of it I received an award at the annual meeting.

If I had prejudged City Hospital and only prospected larger hospitals, another sales rep would have made that sale. If you prejudge men and cherry-pick which ones you go out with, another woman may marry the man of your dreams. You wouldn't want that to happen, would you?

Some women ask me how they can get over the fact that only a certain type of man attracts them. They don't want to prejudge, but the thought of going out with a man who, for example, is shorter than they are, makes them want to give up completely. I tell those women that they are allowed to have one physical turnoff. If height truly bothers them, they can stick to taller men, but they should try to be more flexible about how tall they really need to be. If they typically don't like men under six feet, but they themselves are only five foot four, they should give a little and accept dates with men who are five nine and above.

You are only allowed one physical turnoff, so choose wisely.

Virtually anything physical can also be improved upon. Weight can be lost, clothes can be changed, hair can be cut, and so on and so forth. It's what is on the inside that cannot be so easily changed. I'd take a man with a great heart who could use some hair product and a shave over a GQ model with narcissistic tendencies. It's important to keep in mind what qualities truly matter in the long run and not just what turns you on for the night.

Stop Judging, Start Dating

Three months after my conversation with Megan and Mallory, they were out together at a local pub prospecting again for eligible guys. Megan once again immediately resigned to sitting at a table in the back because there weren't any cute guys out that night. Mallory, on the other hand, kept her mind and options open. As she walked to the bathroom, she noticed a guy at the bar checking her out. He wasn't her typical type, but she decided to not judge. When she came out of the bathroom, she went to the bar to order her next drink, placing herself right next to the guy. She could feel that he was looking her way, so she took a deep breath, smiled, and looked at him.

"Hi! How are you?" he said right away.

"I'm good. I've just been abandoned by my waitress," she laughed.

"Oh, allow me. That looks like a rum and coke?" he smiled.

"Good guess," Mallory replied.

As Megan sat alone at the table, Mallory chatted with the guy for half an hour. He asked for her number and said he would call her. Mallory left the bar that night feeling optimistic. She wasn't sure if the guy was going to be The One, but she liked him more than she thought she would have after their brief conversation.

Today Mallory tells me she has never been so in love. She and Wilson (that's his name) have been dating for almost a year. Although she said he wasn't physically her type at first glance, she finds him very sexy now that she knows him. Whenever they are out, they can't keep their hands off each other, and I have it on good authority that Wilson is planning to propose next month.

Megan on the other hand is still very single and searching.

When you stop judging men from the outside and instead keep yourself open to learning more about them, something wonderful happens. You become attracted to them! Don't let a shallow mentality keep you from meeting great guys. There are tons out there, you just have to be open to getting to know them. If you are prospecting online and think that the men who are contacting you are not physically appealing, keep this in mind: how many times have you been excited by someone's profile only to have them show up in person and completely disappoint you? Well, as many times as that happens, the opposite occurs as well. You can be lukewarm about meeting someone based on their picture and then be pleasantly surprised when you meet face-to-face. You just have to allow for the chance to have that happen.

The next time you decide that someone isn't worth talking to because they aren't tall enough or dressed the right way, ask yourself how you would feel if a man passed you by for the same reason. Give men a chance to show you what else they have to offer. When you factor in a great sense of humor and a great personality, an average-looking guy can suddenly look well above average. Just remember this the next time you prospect: if you stop prejudging, you will start dating.

Filling the Funnel

When my mother recently got involved in real estate, she was very excited. She bought every book, went to every lecture, and committed herself to giving this new venture 100 percent. After a couple of months she found her first clients, a newly married couple. She was eager to sell them a house and focused all her time and energy on this one deal. But after several weeks of searching for that perfect fit, her clients suddenly dropped her. As you can imagine, my mom was pretty upset, but she decided to move on and find another client as quickly as possible. She found a couple that needed to relocate to Virginia by the end of the month. She was once again excited by the possibilities, and this time she was certain she would see results much faster.

But a month later the couple called to tell her they had changed their mind about relocating and would not need her anymore. Once again, she was depressed. It took her a couple days to get back on the horse this time and to begin to look for another client. After a month she still hadn't found anyone. At lunch one day she expressed her disappointment to me.

"I have been at this for almost nine months," she said, "and I am just not seeing any progress. I find clients, I work really hard to help them find a good fit, but ultimately something happens, and it doesn't work out. Now I have to start all over from scratch, and it's really disappointing."

I could sympathize with my mom's frustration. Every sales-person has been in her shoes at some point. However, the good ones have learned what to do to avoid having to start all over again when they lose a sale—they fill the funnel.

I told my mom her main problem was that she only focused on one client at a time, so when that one client fell through, it left her back at square one. Good salespeople don't put all their eggs in one basket; they fill their funnel with lots of sales, knowing that some will not work out. You must keep pros-pecting so that you have enough business to lose a few deals and still be okay.

"Always keep two or three customers in your funnel," I told my mom. "You have to continue to prospect even when you find a potential buyer. You have to keep that funnel full."

Once my mom started juggling a few deals at a time, her sales picked up, and she was making money.

Most of my friends date the way my mom started out sell-ing houses—one prospect at a time. Jane, who is unmarried at thirty-five, admitted that the biggest mistake she ever made was focusing all her efforts on one man from the very start.

"If I could go back and do it all over again" Jane said, "I would have kept my options open until I was in a committed relationship. Whenever I was dating someone and another guy would express interest, I would always say, 'Thanks, but I have a boyfriend,' even though it wasn't true! I had only started see-ing the guy. I assumed he would eventually become my boy-friend, but it was a terrible assumption to make. Looking back on it now I wish I had given those guys a chance. I wish I had gone out to dinner with them once at the very least."

When most women find a guy they like, they immediately cut off all other prospects. They tell me they want to see where the relationship will go and they want to focus all their attention on this one guy, hoping he will be The One. That is risky business, however. Why would you cut off other men when you aren't even sure if this one is going to work out?

Some women do this subconsciously. They don't realize that they close all doors when they start dating someone new. But they do. They don't leave themselves open for other opportunities to come along. Other women simply think they cannot date more than one man at a time. They believe that it is just flat-out wrong. But why? Why is it wrong? Unless the man thinks that you are dating exclusively (and in the beginning stages they definitely don't), I see no problem.

Hopefully, you will only be married once. You are looking for just one guy in a sea of many. It's up to you how quickly (or slowly) it takes you to find him. If you only date one guy at a time, then it will take you a lot longer than if you fill your funnel. It's really the only way to date. I am not saying you should cheat on your wonderful boyfriend and continue to juggle other men on the side. Not at all. I'm saying don't cross your fingers and hope that the guy you've been dating for three weeks will be the one to work out. You don't even know him yet! How can you possibly tell? Salespeople don't stop prospecting when they come across one opportunity to make a sale. They work on closing deals and continue filling the funnel at the same time. That way if one deal falls through, they still have another one to move on to. You have to date the same way or you could be wasting a lot of your time.

Avery, who is twenty-five, had never thought to date more than one man at a time. When she met someone she liked, she naturally assumed that a relationship would follow. But that mentality always took her on a trip to Desperate Town, U.S.A. She would put so much hope and effort into her dates that she would hang on a guy's every word, ignore things that bothered her, and push for a relationship too soon. Every guy she went out with faded away within weeks. Then she started learning my techniques. At first she was skeptical and didn't think she could possibly fill her funnel, but after giving it a try she began to see immediate results. She incidentally stopped her bad habits of texting too much or acting so needy because she wasn't so concerned with one man. Her confidence started to build and she actually began having fun on her dates.

After dating this way for only six months, Avery met the man who would become her husband the following year. She's now happily in love and has the family she has always wanted. She says she owes a large part of her success to keeping her funnel full at all times.

Before I was married, I filled my funnel as well. I would just assume any guy I went out with was seeing other people. We didn't have any conversations about our relationship in the beginning. Why would we? Until the guy had the "relationship

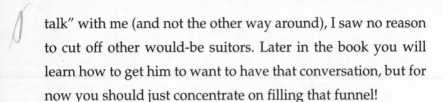

talk" with me (and not the other way around), I saw no reason to cut off other would-be suitors. Later in the book you will learn how to get him to want to have that conversation, but for now you should just concentrate on filling that funnel!

Dating with a Net

Most women ask me how they can avoid becoming attached to a man too soon. Some are hooked after one date or even one kiss. Even though the guy is still a complete stranger, they begin daydreaming about a blissful future as they wait by the phone. My best friend Adison was this way. She was dying to find a boyfriend. So whenever she met someone who showed interest in her, she immediately focused all her time and energy on him.

That's exactly what happened when she found Gavin. She was prospecting the pages of Facebook and she stumbled upon his profile. He was very cute, and after a few short e-sessions, they decided to meet at a restaurant near her house. Dinner was fun, and afterward Adison asked Gavin to come back to her place. They continued to have a good time, and Gavin didn't leave until 3:00 AM.

She called me the following morning and proclaimed her love for her new beau.

"He's so cute and sweet. I just love him. I can't wait to see him again. I hope he calls tonight. I want to take him to my company party on Friday and then to your barbecue on Saturday. I think I'm going to call him and ask him tomorrow if he doesn't call me by tonight."

Adison called him the next day and the day after. They saw each other without a hitch for a couple of weeks. Adison didn't go out with any other guys because she was so into Gavin. She believed that they had something special and she was in it for the long haul. But then suddenly Gavin started to pull away. He didn't always answer Adison's calls and he didn't come over as much. When he did come over she never wanted him to leave because she didn't know when she was going to see him again.

One day at lunch she was telling me how she was checking his Facebook profile and she discovered several pictures of him posted with the same girl.

"I think he's seeing this girl Rachel. I don't know what to do. I texted him last night to come over, but he said he was at his parents' house. So I drove over to his house, and his car was outside. He lied to me. I don't know if I should text him and tell him he's a jerk or if I should call him and talk to him about it."

"Adison, you don't do anything," I reprimanded. "He never said he wanted a relationship with you. He never said you were his girlfriend. You just started acting like you were together. You should have continued to go out with other guys while you were seeing him."

Adison agreed I was right. But it was too late. She had lost Gavin and now her funnel was dry. She was back at square one, and she was not happy about it.

This is not an uncommon scenario. It happens to a lot of women. The smart ones learn from it and decide not to let it happen again. The rest of them continue on this path and wonder, *Why does this keep happening to me?*

If Adison had a couple of guys calling her, this story may have turned out differently. Instead of wasting time driving by Gavin's house, waiting for his calls, and checking his profile on Facebook, she could have been out with someone else. Even if she really only liked Gavin, if she was out on other dates, she wouldn't be home obsessing about him. On top of that, Gavin would have sensed that Adison was busy doing other things and may have kept pursuing her. But she put all her eggs in Gavin's basket, and when he ultimately stopped calling her, she was left completely alone, devastated, and had to start all over again.

To sum it all up, filling the funnel works for several reasons:

❶ You don't get too attached too soon. If you are out with other people then you are not sitting at home thinking about Mr. One-and-Only. You can drive yourself crazy by obsessing about a man, and when you see him again, he'll know you've been pining after him. Believe me, guys aren't dumb. They know.

❷ You won't be a complete wreck if he dumps you. Because you have a couple of different men to date, your confidence won't be shattered if the relationship doesn't pan out. Of course, the initial breakup will still sting, but your ego will be intact because you have other men lusting after you.

❸ Your odds are better. The more men you date, the more likely
you are to find The One. Think about it, you can either date
one man every six months and then in five years you will have
dated ten guys. Or you can date ten guys in one year and in
five years you will have dated fifty guys! The more guys you
date, the closer you get to finding The One.

When you start filling the funnel, a lot of the guys will be
fine with not knowing what you are doing when you aren't
with them . . . at first. But after a while they will begin to wonder. Then they will begin to ask. Then they will begin to worry.
And when a guy worries, that is a good sign for you. (This is
also when the Jones Effect kicks in, which you will learn about
in Chapter 5.)

So remember, ladies, fill the funnel. It's the only way to find
the man of your dreams, and it will help you keep him once
you do.

CHAPTER FIVE

getting him interested

Recognizing Buying Signs

"I just don't understand. He asked for my number, texted me several times, and now he has just disappeared!"

I was sitting on my couch with my new client Penny. She had recently met a guy at a friend's birthday party and was excited to go out with him. The only problem was that after a week and a half of texting, he still hadn't officially asked her out. She had dropped several hints that she was interested in seeing him, but he didn't bite. Fed up, Penny decided to mention that she was going to be in his area and asked if he wanted to grab some lunch. That was the last exchange they had. The guy never texted her again.

"Why do guys do this? Why do they seem interested one minute and then not the next?" she asked.

"I know it's hard to understand, but not all guys who ask for your number are seriously interested in getting to know you," I told her.

"Ouch. That was harsh," Penny replied.

"I'm sorry. What I mean is that you can't just assume that a man is 100 percent interested in dating you just because he asked for your number or flirted with you at a party. Men have different levels of interest. Depending on what kind of guy they are, or what their current situation is, their level of interest can range from high to low," I told her.

"So how am I supposed to know if a man is truly interested in me? I'm tired of feeling disappointed time and time again. Is there a way to know what to expect from someone?" she asked.

"There is a way," I told her. "You have to learn to read a guy's Buying Signs."

People in general won't just come out and tell you their level of interest. You have to learn to read their Buying Signs. Buying Signs are those little subtle indicators that tell you when you are piquing someone's interest. Lots of women don't know how to read a man's Buying Signs and they end up chasing men who are either moderately interested or not that interested at all. They ignore the clear signs, or in this case, lack thereof, and instead of doing certain things to possibly ignite more interest, they simply throw themselves at the guy—killing the small amount of intrigue he had left.

In Penny's case, the guy she had met at the party was only moderately interested in her. He had enjoyed their chat at the party, but he had also met two other girls that same night. Over the course of the week he texted with each girl, but Penny was the most responsive. She was so excited to have a potential prospect that she didn't notice when the guy's texts started slowing down and he became less engaging. Eventually he decided that he was more interested and more compatible with another girl and simply moved on to focus on her instead. Even though he was interested the night he met Penny, the interest didn't sustain. Penny just assumed it would, which is why she was so disappointed. She had set the expectation that she would date the guy and eventually get into a relationship with him—a common assumption that often leads to a letdown.

Reading the Signs

Guys will never flat-out tell you just how interested they are. You have to figure out their level of interest on your own. I was always under the impression that a man's feelings were black and white. He either liked me or he didn't. It wasn't until much later that I realized there was a huge gray area. A man's interest can range from high to low, and learning to read his signs of interest will ultimately help you better set your expectations.

Reading Buying Signs may also save you a bit of humiliation. When I was a freshman in college, I was gaga over Zach Palamino. (No, that's not his real name, so don't go Googling him.) He was a few years older than I was, and every time I ran into him on campus, I started to hyperventilate. One night at a frat party my friend grabbed him and made him dance with me. I was over the moon. He was slightly intoxicated, but I didn't care. I spent the rest of the night talking to him and he even walked me to my car and asked for my number.

After that night, I saw him a few times on campus. He would always stop and talk to me, but never said anything about going out. He never called either. I was plagued with distress. Why would he ask for my number and then not call? Why wasn't he asking me out?

One night I decided to take matters into my own hands. So I called him. He answered the phone and talked to me for roughly three minutes. Then he said his roommate needed to use the phone and he would call me back. He never did.

Looking back on it now, I realized that Zach started out only moderately interested, and the actions I took from there made him even less interested. When I saw him on campus I went out of my way to run into him. I ended every conversation mentioning that he should call me. I even had a friend talk to him for me. Pathetic, I know. One night while drinking at a local bar, I told him how hot I thought he was and tried to kiss him. At the time I saw nothing wrong with my actions. I told myself he was just shy and I needed to be more aggressive. Now when

I think about it, my face gets redder than a tomato. How could I have been so oblivious? How did I not read the signs?

The truth is I didn't want to read the signs. I wanted to ignore them! I was so crazy about Zach that accepting he may not like me was something I couldn't face. And because he never verbally said he was not interested, I continued to believe he was. He danced with me one night at a party and walked me to my car so I thought it was love. Wouldn't you?

The Gray Area

I remember nearly losing my mind trying to figure out Zach. Some people call it mixed messages when a guy asks for your number, but then doesn't call. Or he calls you, but not regularly. He may be all over you one night, but not the next. It's up to you to understand and interpret these signs. He's not going to spell it out for you—but I will. You are in the gray area, and these are not mixed messages. These are clear signs of moderate to low interest.

Before I met my husband I experienced another classic case of low interest from a guy. Had I not been good at interpreting Buying Signs by then, I could have easily wasted my time. It all started while I was checking my profile on Facebook. I got a friend request from an extremely handsome Orlando Bloom look-alike. I was totally surprised and excited as I read his profile. He was a young doctor who seemed to have a great sense of humor. I decided to post a comment on his page saying thanks for the friend request. I waited a couple of days to check to see if he would respond. To my disappointment he didn't. I decided to let it go; after all, what could I really do at that point? A couple months went by and I had almost forgotten about Orlando. But as I was checking my profile on my birthday, I realized he had posted another comment. I was elated and rejuvenated. He was definitely digging me, or so I thought. I gave it a day, posted a comment back, and waited for a response. Nothing. No reply. I was perplexed. I wanted to meet this guy. He seemed so interesting, not to mention gorgeous. All my friends urged me to e-mail and ask him out. They kept reminding me that he was the one who found me and initiated contact. I went back and forth about what to do. I knew what they were saying was true, but I also knew that his Buying Signs were telling me he was only moderately interested, if that. Being persistent would not heighten his level of interest. So against my friends' advice I decided to go with what my head was telling me. I didn't write him again.

The following week I decided to go to a restaurant opening in Chinatown. As I walked toward the mass of people swarming the entrance, I saw the same dark curly hair that was driving me to insanity. It was him. Orlando! He was in line waiting to get in. I walked right up to the door because I happened to know the owner, and strolled right by him. As I stood by the bar talking to friends, I eagerly waited for him to walk through the door. After what seemed like hours, he finally did. But he was not alone. On his arm was a tall brunette he clearly knew very well. As he leaned on the bar to order drinks, she stuck her hand deep into his back pocket. *Girlfriend,* I thought. *Definitely the girlfriend.*

I was very glad that I didn't continue to e-mail Orlando. He was less than moderately interested, like I originally thought. I later discovered he and his girlfriend had been dating for two years. They could have been in a fight when he contacted me, or perhaps he was just a cheater and some other girl jumped on his friend request when I didn't. Either way, there was not any real interest on his part. Continuing contact with him would have been the wrong thing to do. He was clearly in a relationship and the only thing to do was wait to see what happened next. Maybe they would break up, maybe they wouldn't. But I had done my part.

Unfortunately, most of the time you aren't going to find out what's happening on the other side like I did. You are going to have to read the signs and determine for yourself what a man's interest level is. I was lucky enough to get a sneak peek, but that doesn't happen very often. You have to be smart enough to read the signs and act accordingly. I could have easily kept e-mailing Orlando, thinking he was interested, but it would have backfired on me. He had a girlfriend, and the ball was not in my court.

It may drive you nuts not knowing why someone isn't crazy over you, but the reason doesn't matter anyway. In the beginning, you must trust that it is nothing you have control over and act according to the signs you're reading. If you don't, and you push yourself into a relationship with a man whose level of interest is beneath your own, he won't love you; he'll just use you. Then you will be sucked into something that will never satisfy you and could possibly devastate you.

The Initial Signs of Interest

Gauging a man's interest in the beginning is pretty simple, as there are definitely standard Buying Signs that every man uses. The first is the look. If a man is interested in meeting you, you will catch his eye. It's the same thing that happens when you walk through the mall. If you see a dress or a pair of shoes you like, what do you do? You stop and look. Some men try not to make it obvious; others are rather overt about it. Needless to say, when someone is interested in buying, they first stop and look.

The second sign of interest is questioning. When a customer is interested in a product, they ask a lot of questions. They want to know as much as they can about that product in the little time they have. Think about when you try on a dress at the mall. If you like it, you ask questions like, "How much is it? Does it come in my size? Are there any other colors?" Men are no different. They will ask you questions about yourself if they are interested. He will want to know who you are, what you do, where you live, and anything else he can think of. If he does not ask you anything and proceeds to ramble on about himself and his interest, read the signs. He is more interested in himself than you.

The third sign is change in attitude and mannerisms. When a customer is interested in buying, he may suddenly change his tone of voice, attitude, or posture. He may become friendlier or chattier. When a man is interested in a woman, he will do exactly the same thing. He will maintain strong eye contact while engaging in deeper conversation. As time passes, he may become more touchy-feely. His tone and body language will make it apparent that he is interested.

The fourth and final sign of interest is probably the most obvious. When a customer is interested they basically tell you before you can even ask. They make closing statements like, "That sounds good," or "Where do I sign?" A man won't say those things exactly, or at least let's hope not, but he will say things that reference seeing you again. I once met a guy at my gym who asked me where I usually went running. When I told him the specific trail, he said he often runs there too and we should run it together sometime. That is a closing statement. If he doesn't come out and ask you for a date on the first meeting, you should not be discouraged. Most guys want to wait and see if they get a Buying Sign from you before asking for your number. Listen for other closing statements that tell you he wants to see you again, and then let him know you would be receptive to it by maintaining a good strong SEE Factor (see Chapter 4) and saying yes when he attempts to suggest a possible date.

The Signs of Low to Moderate Interest

After you've met and maybe even gone on a few dates, it will be a lot easier to tell what his interest level is. If he calls you a lot, sends you texts every day, tries constantly to see you, he's very interested. Anything less than that is moderate to not-that-interested. Doesn't matter what the extenuating circumstances are. A stressful job, a heavy travel schedule, a recent breakup—they are all just excuses. If he's not sending you a clear signal of high interest, it's because he's not that interested . . . at least not yet. You can certainly change his level, but you have to first be honest with yourself and realize that you may be more into him than he is into you.

If you don't hear from a man for days and making plans only happens on his terms, read the signs. Moderate interest. If you only hang out with his friends, at his house, and doing what he wants, again, moderate interest. If he only calls you when he's out, drunk, and late at night . . . do I really need to tell you what that means?

There's no such thing as mixed messages. The signs are very clear. The only problem is with you, the interpreter. It can be tough to face the fact that the man you are pining after may not be as interested in you as you want him to be. But if you make excuses for his wishy-washy behavior, you are only kidding yourself. Everyone else, including your friends, knows exactly what's happening, even if they don't tell you.

Starting High, but Ending Low

Unfortunately, just because someone expresses initial interest doesn't mean you're guaranteed to close them on a relationship. Sometimes customers start off extremely interested in a product, but somewhere in the sales process, their interest wanes. The worst part about that is that they'll sometimes continue to act interested just to be nice. Sometimes they just want free pens, and sometimes they want to be taken to lunch. There are several reasons why an uninterested customer will string a salesperson along, so we have to look for signs that indicate that the customer is serious about buying and does not have an ulterior motive.

After you've been dating awhile, you have to be careful a guy doesn't do the same thing to you. You have to continue to read his signs throughout your entire courtship to be sure his interest is holding and also to be certain he doesn't have a less honorable agenda. Remember, just because he initially asked for your number or told you that you turned every head in the room doesn't mean he's in love with you. Unfortunately, there are men who are only out for sex and don't care who they hurt in order to get it.

Adison often makes the mistake of assuming when a guy asks for her number he is totally smitten with her and therefore she can act any way she wants. She throws her strategy out the window and ignores all other signs. She figures he made the first move, so she has the upper hand. She doesn't think twice about anything she says or does. Then when the guy breaks off the relationship, she's left baffled. "He asked for my number!" she cries. "He chased *me!*" She has a hard time accepting that just because a man's interest starts out high doesn't mean it will stay that way. A man's interest is like the weather. It can drop from high to low overnight.

It's important to read a man's Buying Signs, whether they are sky-high or valley low. Your actions can affect his level of interest, so don't despair if the outlook seems gloomy at the moment. It is very possible to turn him around. But first you have to read and accept the signs, so that you know where you stand. Learn the signs of someone really liking you. Learn the signs when someone only moderately likes you. And most important, learn the signs of when someone doesn't really like you but because you are readily available, they use you when they want to. Don't make excuses for rotten behavior. If a man is truly interested and is thinking about a serious relationship with you, there will be clear signs telling you so. If he's not there yet, don't worry. The rest of this book is going to teach you how to get him interested and keep him that way.

The KISS Principle

My good friend Aidan relies heavily on blind dates. He's a smart but quiet guy who doesn't go out much, and prefers to be set up through friends. He figures they know his likes and dislikes, so having them choose his dates for him should be a safe bet. However, the last date he went on had him really doubting his friends' ability.

The night got off to a great start when Aidan's date walked in exactly the way she had been described. She was a cute brunette with a curvaceous figure and a dazzling smile. *Jackpot!* he thought to himself. He was instantly pleased and ready for an enjoyable evening. Unfortunately, not long after they ordered their first drinks, the good start came to a screeching halt.

She asked Aidan what he did for a living.

"I own a wine store," he said.

"Oh my God, really?" she exclaimed. "I love wine. I have been to a lot of the vineyards in the area. I use to be a waitress at this restaurant on Capitol Hill, and they wanted the staff to be familiar with all the wines so we could accurately describe them to the patrons. There were so many wines that it was hard for everyone to remember them all, but I must have a nose for wine because I could just smell the wine and know exactly what was in it. Everyone thought it was amazing actually."

Aidan raised his brow, "Well, that's cool."

"Do you like sports?" the girl asked.

"Uh, I do. I'm not as into them as I used to be, but I do follow my favorite teams," Aidan said.

"Oh, me too! I mean, I do like sports, like football and soccer are okay, but I'm not married to them. I can sit down and watch them with my boyfriend if that's what he wants to do, but I don't have to be in front of the TV every Monday night for the Skins' game. It's something that I can take or leave myself. I actually played field hockey when I was in high school, so I am pretty athletic. The year I was the cocaptain we won the regional championship. Gosh, that was so long ago, now that I think about it . . ."

Again Aidan raised his brow, then looked down at his watch.

After forty-five minutes passed, he finally told the girl that he forgot to lock the back door at the store and had to go. She hugged him good-bye and told him she had fun. He lied and said the same thing.

When Aidan called me the next day, I asked him about the date. He only had one thing to say.

"She talked too much. We're not going out again."

"Oh? What was it she was talking about exactly?" I asked.

"Mainly herself," he replied. "She started off pretty good. She seemed interested in getting to know me, but then whenever I answered her questions, she would immediately come up with a story that related back to her. It got very annoying."

"Well, she was probably trying to show you that you and she have a lot in common. She just went about it the wrong way."

"Maybe, but at this point I don't care what her intention was. I'm not putting myself through that again," Aidan said firmly. "She was just agreeing with everything I said anyway. The conversation was not interesting at all. She also cut me off a few times, so it's obvious she likes to hear herself talk. It's too bad because she was very attractive and I would have gone out with her again. Oh well, on to the next."

Aidan's date started out doing the right thing. She asked questions. At first she seemed genuinely interested in Aidan. But as soon as he answered her question, she would jump in and ramble on and on about her own stories, always turning the conversation back to herself. Many girls I know unwittingly do the same thing. They go on dates and talk way too much. They are so worried about impressing the guy that they talk themselves right out of a relationship. It's a disease I call "verbal vomit." There is no faster way to kill a potential relationship than to verbal vomit on your date. You may think you are keeping the conversation going by telling your funny and agreeable stories, but from the guys' perspective you just come off looking like a motormouth.

KISS Your Date

People often think that salespeople are great talkers. But it's not the talking that makes them great. Just the opposite. The real secret is that salespeople are great listeners. They spend time really getting to know their customers and listening to what they have to say. This makes the customer feel special and cared about, something that is absolutely necessary when they are deciding to make a purchase. Whenever I would visit with a potential buyer, I would make sure that they were the ones doing most of the talking. My rule was they talk 75 percent of the time and I talk 25 percent of the time. The last thing I wanted to do was to monopolize the conversation and bore the customer. I know that people love to talk, and they lose interest fast when they are just sitting there listening to my pitch. I have to engage them, just like you have to engage your dates. Men especially have short attention spans. After a few minutes of listening to you, you have to let him talk. If you drone on, they will lose interest in what you are saying and then lose interest in you. Remember, we have two ears and one mouth for a reason!

It is more important to connect with your date, rather than impress him, so instead of trying to "wow" a guy with your wit or sense of humor, simply be that girl who is easy to talk to. The best thing you can do on a date is to ask a guy questions about himself. You can always keep the conversation going with questions, and you will make your date feel like you are genuinely interested in him as a person. When it's your turn to talk, use the same principle salespeople have been using for years: the KISS Principle. It stands for keep it short and simple. Using KISS will help keep you from babbling and ensure that your date has a good time with you. It's also the only cure for verbal vomit.

When I was in my twenties I remember going on a first date with a local TV newscaster. I was a little nervous and not sure what we were going to talk about. He seemed much older and far worldlier than me. Then I remembered that all I needed to do was ask him questions and keep my answers short and simple. We sat at a restaurant bar for two hours, but the conversation never stalled because I continually asked him questions about himself, his family, his career, his aspirations. Whenever he asked me a question, I would KISS the answer, and then turn the attention back to him. By the time the date ended and he walked me to my car, he turned to me and said, "You are one of the most interesting people I have ever met. I just love talking to you!"

It's funny—when you let someone else do the talking, you are the one who seems interesting.

A good quality guy will recognize when he has been doing all the talking, and will always turn the conversation back to you. A man who continues to talk about himself as if he were the most interesting man on Earth is probably someone you don't want to go on a second date with, in my opinion.

Verbal Vomit with a Headache

Because women are such emotional creatures, it's often hard for us to keep what we're thinking from coming out of our mouths. If we are nervous, we say we are nervous. If we can't believe a guy asked us out, we'll actually tell him we can't believe he asked us out. Unfortunately, it's not always a good idea to disclose all the thoughts dancing around in our heads. Just because you are thinking it doesn't mean you should be talking about it. Especially on a first date.

There are certain things that shouldn't be discussed when you are starting to get to know someone. For instance, you shouldn't discuss personal problems that you aren't exactly over yet. When you complain about a bad situation at home, work, or anywhere else, you could end up giving your date something I call verbal vomit with a headache.

My good friend Isabel recently went through the hardest year of her life. She had bought a second condo as an investment property even though her gut was telling her she couldn't afford it. After several months of trying to rent it without success, she decided to put it up for sale. The real estate agent she hired assured her they would get a good deal for it, but as the months progressed she had to keep lowering the price. Finally, after having it on the market for almost a year, she went into foreclosure.

I've never seen my poor friend such a wreck. Of course, she bounced back, but it took a toll on her emotionally. When she started dating again she was still mentally exhausted from the experience. She said she had a migraine every day that year, and she let her dates know it, too. If a guy brought up anything relating to the housing market, Isabel would unload all her frustration right on his plate. She would tell him how angry she was and how she wanted to strangle her agent. She complained about not being able to eat or sleep and thought she may need therapy due to the whole ordeal. A couple of times, Isabel even ended up crying about it. Her dates sat there not knowing exactly what to say and feeling very uncomfortable.

In the beginning, you really should keep the personal strife in your life private. I know women who talk about their abusive father, eating disorders, pregnancy scares, medication they take, health problems they've had, and a million other things that are meant for a therapist, not a first date. If you really want to scare a man off, then go ahead and air all your dirty laundry. But if you want to keep seeing a guy, learn to keep the personal problems to yourself for the time being. When he tells you he had the flu and couldn't leave the house for a week, don't tell him about the year you couldn't get out of bed because of your clinical depression. It's okay to get personal, as long as you are discussing happy topics, but either way you should still keep the focus on him. Continue to ask him questions about himself, and be sure to KISS all your answers.

KISS Me Through the Phone

My client Mary Beth had a lot of trouble using the KISS Principle. She loved to talk and tell men exactly what was on her mind. After several botched dates, however, she realized that disclosing all her thoughts and feelings was not helping her to build relationships. In fact, it was hurting her significantly. She decided she needed to stop verbal vomiting and went to great lengths in order to let the guys talk more than she did. At first, everything was going well and most of her first dates were calling for seconds and thirds. A huge improvement! Then all of a sudden her success came to a screeching halt. Men who were pursuing her like crazy suddenly lost interest after date three. I didn't know what to think at first, but then I saw a few e-mails and texts on Mary Beth's phone and it was all the evidence I needed. She may have mastered KISS in person, but on the phone she was still a wordy wreck. All her e-mails and texts were longer and much more verbose than her would-be dates. If they sent a simple, "How was your day?" text, she would respond with detailed information about everything that had happened in the last eight hours. On the phone, Mary Beth wasn't *KISS*ing her dates—she was *KILL*ing them.

The KISS Principle isn't something you only use when you are face-to-face with a guy; it's a method to use with any form of communication. You have to remember that in the beginning, you are in the getting-to-know-you phase and texting or e-mailing too much can make the other person feel as if you are rushing the relationship. Why else would you be talking so much to a person you don't know yet? Slow down and pace yourself when it comes to chatting with boys. They want to get to know you, but it has to happen at a gradual pace, otherwise they may abruptly stop contacting you on their own. Overtexting is a bad habit that you have to work to break, so it's better just to try and avoid forming it in the first place. Keep your texts and e-mails short and simple, regardless of how long and lengthy a guy gets. Yes, it is a sign of high interest when a man is constantly contacting you, but remember you can easily kill that interest by responding in a disproportionate manner.

Don't KISS and Tell—KISS and Listen

When you are excited about someone, it's easy to ramble. You are making a connection and bursting to tell him all the things you're thinking. But what makes a person like you has less to do with what you say and more to do with how you make them feel. People like to feel that they are being heard. They like to feel like their voice matters. Keep that in mind when you are on your dates. Making a good impression isn't tough, if you know how to listen.

Verbal vomit comes in many forms. Some women are just chatty. Some are afraid of the awkward silence. Some think that the only way for a guy to realize how great they are is to just flat-out tell him, "Hey, I'm great." Whatever form it comes in doesn't really matter. All that does matter is keeping it under control and focusing on getting to know the guy you are with. Sit back, relax, and remember if you don't KISS your date, you will kill it.

End at the Height of Impulse

When my friend Anne moved to San Francisco, she didn't know a soul. I admired her strength to pick up and move three thousand miles from home, but I also worried about how she would meet people and regain her social life. After only being out West a few months, she decided to join Match .com. It seemed like the best way to meet guys and get back on the social scene. She posted her profile and began receiving e-mails immediately. After sorting through a slew of messages, she decided to make a date with Patrick, a sous-chef from Los Angeles. He was tall, dark, and handsome with a seemingly good sense of humor. They decided to meet on a Friday night and get a couple of drinks. Now remember as I tell you this story, Anne and Patrick had never met before. In fact, they hadn't even spoken on the phone.

When Anne walked in and saw Patrick, she was immediately pleased. He was exactly what his profile had stated—yummy! Patrick was excited to meet Anne, too. He thought she was gorgeous. The first encounter was a success. They got a few drinks and the night began.

After their third round, Patrick suggested they get some dinner. They left the bar and headed to a nice restaurant on the Bay. Dinner was delicious and Anne and Patrick were engrossed in conversation for the next three hours. They decided to then go for a walk on the beach. Patrick picked up some champagne and glasses, and they headed out for a midnight picnic. By now Patrick and Anne had been drinking for hours and inhibitions were long gone. They started making out on the beach, and Anne eventually ended up at Patrick's, where they continued to make out until six in the morning.

The next day Anne was beaming. It was the perfect first date. She was extremely excited and even called to tell me about it. Just as she was in the middle of the story, her other line beeped. "It's him!" she squealed. "Let me call you right back." She clicked over and didn't call me for two days.

Those two days she didn't call back she spent with Patrick. Basically their first date started Friday and didn't end until Sunday. The following week Patrick called and asked to see her again. She accepted, of course, and spent that entire weekend with him as well. At some point during their multinight slumber party, they consummated their relationship. Her rationale? She felt like she knew him after spending so much time with him, even if it was only in the span of two weeks. Things were going exactly the way she wanted. She was happy.

Then came the third week, which also became known as the final week. That's when things got rocky. I'll skip the unimportant details, but by week three the happy couple was no longer a couple, and Anne was calling me crying and cursing his name. I tried to console her, but eventually I had to tell her that she had done something terribly wrong. She spent way too much time with Patrick in the beginning of the relationship. If it was going so well, she should have pulled back a little more. She shouldn't have said yes every time he asked her out, and she should have cut the dates shorter. Every time she went out with Patrick, they spent at least twelve hours together. It was relationship overkill, and it destroyed the happy ending they might have had.

Saying No

Even though Patrick kept pursuing Anne and asking her out, she shouldn't have always accepted. Just because a guy asks you a question doesn't mean you are required to come back with an affirmative answer. It's perfectly fine to turn a guy down, and in many instances you may have to in order to keep his interest in the very beginning. "No" is not a dirty word in dating. It's important not to overexpose yourself by seeing the guy too much in the first couple of months. Even if you are totally falling in love, and he wants to see you every day, in the very beginning, you have to keep a guy wanting more. There is a simple yet effective way to accomplish this, and that is to leave him when things are at their most exciting. It's called "Ending at the Height of Impulse." You want to end every date at the appropriate time so that the guy is still thinking about you when you're gone.

All Good Things Must Come to an End, Quickly

You've seen it before, and it always works. It's why soap operas end at the most exciting point of the show. It's why *Sex and the City* ended after only six short seasons, and why George Costanza exited every meeting after a great joke. You always want to leave on a high note. Similarly, you have to leave a man wanting more, and you can't do that if you never leave. You will have to restrain yourself from spending too much time with a guy in the very beginning. Even if he gets down on his knees and begs you to stay, that is the time that you absolutely need to go.

I know this is hard to do. When you meet a guy who you actually like, and you are feeling good about how things are going, the last thing you want to do is go home. But it truly is the only way to keep him interested. I don't care if you found your soul mate and he's different from all the other guys. Don't let your heart confuse you. If you spend too much time with him right away, he can and will get burned out.

The Danger of Losing Impulse

Back when I was a brand-new sales rep selling phone service, I walked into a lawyer's office in a small town in southern Virginia. I asked for the head attorney who made all the decisions for the office. I was surprised when they immediately took me back to see him.

His name was Sully. He was a great big man with a great big laugh. He shook my hand and told me to have a seat. He was more than willing to hear what I had to say. I was excited as I gave him my spiel. I knew this deal was in the bag from the Buying Signs he was giving me. Sully broke out the phone bill and we started going over it. He said he was impressed at how much money I could save him. He kept nodding his head yes and told me that the deal sounded great. Right there—that is the Height of Impulse. That is when I should have ended the conversation, pulled out the contract, and closed the deal.

But instead I kept talking. I was enjoying sitting there, building a relationship with him. We got off the subject a couple of times, talking mainly about his kids and his love of fishing. At one point, we even stepped out of the office so that Sully could get in a quick smoke. Eventually I glanced at the clock and realized I had been there for almost two and a half hours. Usually these visits only took about forty-five minutes. I couldn't waste anymore time. Just as I was about to break out my pen and have Sully put his signature on the deal, he looked at his watch.

"I have to run, Jessica. This deal sounds good, but I just need to think about it a little bit longer. I have to run to a meeting now. Come back next month and see me. We'll talk then."

I was crushed. But it was my fault. Had I just closed him when he was at the Height of Impulse, I would have made the sale. But instead I just kept sitting there, talking, letting his impulse drop. When I finally tried to close him, he was no longer excited about the offer. He was just drained from talking for two hours and late for his next meeting.

If you want to turn a new relationship into a long-term one, you are going to have to make Ending at the Height of Impulse a religious practice. Until a guy tells you that he is crazy about you, and you get all the right Buying Signs from him, you should never spend more than a few hours with him. Doesn't matter how much you like him and how hard it is to leave him, do it. Do it because it's the only way to get what you want.

After Anne got over Patrick, she got back on Match.com. She understood what she had done wrong and swore on a stack of Bibles she wouldn't do it again. Her next date was with Cyrus, a mortgage broker who had also moved out West from D.C. He and Anne planned to meet for coffee. Since it was their first meeting, I advised her to keep it short and simple, no matter how well it was going.

Two hours into the date Anne thought about her promise.

But just as she was getting ready to thank Cyrus for a good time, he asked her if she wanted to get some dinner with him. She didn't want to say no, mostly because she was having such a good time, but also because she didn't want to be rude. What if she turned him down and he became discouraged? What if he never asked her out again? So instead of going home like she should have, she went out to dinner.

Three hours later Anne and Cyrus were drunk, half-naked, and back at his place. They fooled around until two in the morning. Anne didn't want to repeat the Patrick situation, so she sobered up and drove home instead of sleeping over. But by then, she had already sealed her fate. Cyrus saw her two more times and then never called again.

I know it's difficult to End at the Height of Impulse, so here's what I suggest. Before you go on a date, make a promise to yourself that you are not going to stay past a certain time. If it's a first date, say good night at ten or eleven. If you happen to be on an Internet date, I would limit yourself to only one hour, or two cups of coffee. It's always better to leave earlier than later, especially when you are just meeting someone for the first time. As the relationship progresses, keep setting time limits—and make sure you do it before you get there and start having a good time.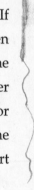

Once, I was dating an attorney who was also labeled an eternal bachelor. He was a night owl and loved to stay out until the wee hours of the morning. On our third date he took me out to dinner and wanted to stop by a local hot spot where his friends were partying. I had already planned to leave him no later than midnight, so when the clock struck twelve, I told him I was catching a cab home. He, of course, was stunned to hear this. How could I leave in the middle of a party? He begged me not to go. He said he would have his driver take me home anytime I wanted. I told him I had to get up early and couldn't stay any later. With that, I turned and slipped out the back door.

I was having a great time, but I had a long-term goal. I wanted the attorney to fall head over heels for me. And in order to do that I needed to make sure he kept wanting me even after I left. He never understood why I always left him around midnight. He started calling me Cinderella and asked if he bought me some really expensive Jimmy Choos would I stay out longer? He called me constantly and even consulted my friends about our relationship. Funny enough, the more he pressured, the less interested I became. But nonetheless, the technique worked!

The Impulse Killer

Perhaps the easiest and most fatal trap to fall into is spending the night. You can't possibly End at the Height of Impulse if you spend the night with your date. If you are sleeping over at his house (or he's sleeping at yours) after only two or three dates, you will kill any impulse he has to see you again. Now, if he's your boyfriend who you have been seeing for several months, that's a slightly different story. But even then, you still shouldn't spend every night with him. It's important to let boyfriends miss you too.

When my client Mary Beth finally perfected her KISS Principle and began dating someone, she had been practicing Ending at the Height of Impulse for quite some time. Jonathan was a thirty-four-year-old owner of a graphic design company who liked Mary Beth right away. He asked her to dinner twice before having her over to his house for a home-cooked meal. After enjoying dinner and killing two bottles of wine, Jonathan asked Mary Beth to stay over. As much as she wanted to, she politely said no. Jonathan was a little dumbfounded at first and began listing all the reasons she should stay, including the fact that he didn't want her to drive home drunk. She agreed that was a bad idea, so she picked up the phone and called a cab.

Mary Beth made the right move. Jonathan called her the very next morning asking if he could take her to breakfast and bring her back to her car.

Mary Beth didn't spend the night with Jonathan for almost two months. It wasn't until Jonathan asked her to be his girlfriend that she finally obliged and stayed over at his house. Ending at the Height of Impulse paid off in dividends.

It is much too hard to resist the urge to sleep over if you haven't already made the promise to yourself that you are going home. Don't do what most girls do. They tell themselves they will make a decision later in the evening after seeing how they feel. The problem is that it always feels good! It never feels like you should go home. But that is exactly the point when you should put your shoes on and skedaddle.

It's vital to a salesperson's success to know when to close a customer. Close too late and they get bored and start to wish you would just leave. There is a reason the saying is "timing is everything" and not "timing is most things." Timing really is everything, and it is within your control. Even if he is singing your praises, you have to resist the urge to stay. If he is begging you not to leave, that just means you are doing the right thing. Don't deviate from the strategy. If you can discipline yourself to go when the going gets hot, you will see just how hot a guy gets going!

Indifference

Ever wonder why so many married women say, "When I met my husband, I wasn't even interested in him." Or, "I would have never noticed my husband, but he chased me down and made me go out with him." It's funny to hear stories like that, but it's also very telling.

When my friend Julie was single she was trying desperately to date her future husband's best friend. It was a classic triangle. George, her future husband, was in love with her, and she was in love with his best friend, Layne. Julie wasn't interested in George, but she liked him a lot as a friend. They would have lunch, go shopping, or just hang out and talk. George could see how smart, funny, and wonderful Julie was because she wasn't trying to date him. She didn't come on strong and hang on his every word. She didn't rush to answer his every text. She wasn't worried if she had to decline an invitation, and wasn't afraid to say no to him. She was indifferent. She liked hanging out with him but she didn't feel like she was going to die if she didn't see him. And because she didn't have romantic feelings for him, she never got mad at him for not calling on time or going out with other girls. That natural indifference was what enabled George to see Julie for who she really was, and allowed him to fall in love with her.

Now if you ask Layne, he will tell you he saw a very different girl in Julie. This girl was not indifferent. Quite the opposite. She always seemed to pop up wherever he was and constantly vied for his attention. If there was ever an opportunity to hang out with him, she made sure she was there. She tried everything she could think of to get Layne to like her. But it didn't work. Layne perceived Julie as clingy and flat-out annoying and thus was never able to see the good qualities George did. After many months of cat and mouse, George finally convinced Julie to give up on Layne and give him a chance. After dating for two years, Julie and George got married. They now have an adorable little boy and she is pregnant again.

Some women end up marrying men they aren't initially interested in because they are naturally indifferent with them in the early stages. They are essentially able to be themselves instead of googly-eyed teenagers, high on emotion. They don't show the guy their deep-rooted feelings early on, simply because they don't have any! But you don't have to marry the guy who wears you down. You can learn how to close the deal with the guy you like right away.

Neediness

Before we talk about how and why it's important to be indifferent with the guy you really like, we need to understand why you may have such a difficult time doing it. The answer can be summed up in one word: neediness. If you are needy, you cannot possibly be indifferent. Neediness is, without a doubt, the most unattractive quality a woman can display.

What exactly is neediness? It is obvious to the most casual observer but often not to a needy woman. Ask yourself these questions: Have you ever been afraid to confront your boyfriend about something that bothers you? Do you always do what he wants to do? Do you make yourself available for him at any cost? Is it okay that he never says how he feels about you, or tells you he loves you? Do you compromise on the things that you want the most? If you have answered yes to these things, you could very well be needy. A great example is my friend Ebony. After telling me for years that she wanted to get married and have children, she decided that she really didn't want to when her boyfriend told her that living together and getting a dog was the same thing, minus the hassle. That is what I call needy.

Most needy women don't even realize that they are needy. Never have any of my needy clients admitted to me that they need a relationship to be happy, but their actions prove the contrary. They can start off strong, but somewhere in the dating process they lose their independence. The indifferent attitude suddenly dissipates, and they become desperate for the guy to like them.

The first thing you have to do is ask yourself if you are needy. You can't solve a problem if you can't admit you have one in the first place. Most women believe that because they have good jobs and make their own money that they are independent, and therefore, are certainly not needy. But neediness has nothing to do with financial instability. It is an emotional insecurity that some women mistakenly think can be fixed by a relationship.

So how can you tell if you are one of the needy ones? If you have ever said one of the following phrases, either out loud or to yourself, you may be a needy girl:

"I think if I were married or had a boyfriend, I would be happier."

"I just don't like being single."

"I am a 'relationship person.' I just like being in a relationship."

"I fall in love very easily."

While these are some examples of things that women will say, more often than not it's what they do that pegs them as needy. If you are the kind of person who is *always* in a serious relationship, then you could be needy. I have friends that "relationship hop," meaning when they detect that their serious relationship is on the decline, they immediately run out and find another serious relationship to jump into. They don't want to date casually or fill the funnel because they like the security that comes with a long-term boyfriend. Relationship hoppers get seriously involved very quickly. They move at the speed of light, taking the relationship from zero to sixty in a matter of weeks. Most hoppers think it's a good sign if the relationship moves this fast, but the reality is that they have now committed themselves to a man they hardly know. As the relationship progresses, the hopper may realize the guy is not exactly what she thought he was, but she can't bring herself to end things and go back to being single. She may not have the relationship she wants, but at least she has a relationship.

Most everyone will admit that they prefer being in a relationship. At some point in life, everyone dreams of finding true love. So hoping to find the man of your dreams does not necessarily mean that you are needy. The difference between people with a healthy understanding of relationships and needy people is that needy people are willing to compromise and rationalize a subpar relationship because they would rather not be alone. They may tell themselves that it's their fault that things aren't going well. They are too critical or nitpicky. They often become the unhappiest of people because they are not in the right relationship, and it is not fulfilling their real needs. These are all signs of neediness, and if they sound familiar to you, it may be time to accept it and start dealing with it.

It's very important to understand that a relationship is not a solution to a problem. Many women think they would be happy if they were married or at least seriously involved with someone. Inevitably, women who think this way find out what true unhappiness really is. Instead of being single and alone, five years later they end up divorced, with a two-year-old, no job, and single again. A relationship based on neediness does not solve problems; it compounds them.

If you are depending on a man to make you happy, think about what kind of pressure that puts on him. No guy is going to want to be with a woman who cannot be happy on her own. The truth is that almost every woman has the ability to take care of herself and find fulfillment. Before you can find a man to share your life with, you will absolutely have to learn to be happy by yourself. It may take extensive coaching or even therapy to get you to that place, but I encourage you to work on whatever specific issues may be keeping you from feeling happy with yourself and your life. If you don't get to the core of the issue and address it head on, you will never find yourself in a truly fulfilling relationship. In the meantime, I can tell you how to act so that you don't seem needy and end up scaring off a great guy—or worse, locking yourself into a bad relationship.

The Most Powerful Tool You Have

There is an old sales story about indifference. Back in the late eighties, two computer salesmen from competing companies went to a large technology convention. They set up their booths across from each other and prepared themselves for a busy day. The convention was packed with people. Many wandered by and glanced at the salesmen's displays, but no one stopped to ask any questions. Back then, hardly anyone owned a computer and no one thought they could afford it. Finally, after a long day of no prospects, the convention ended. Both salesmen were disappointed. Not a single person stopped by either of their booths.

Just as they started to pack up, two women approached the first salesperson's booth. At long last, a potential buyer! The salesperson was so excited. After a long day of standing on his feet, he had an opportunity to make a sale. He thought about how much he needed the money, and he eagerly made his presentation. He told the ladies that they wouldn't regret purchasing his product. Satisfaction was guaranteed! When they said they were going to think about it, the salesperson became even more desperate. He didn't want to lose his only prospect of the day. He began to reiterate the value of his computer and how much he would appreciate their business.

But his enthusiasm didn't convince them. The ladies thanked the first salesperson and walked away from his booth. The second salesperson had watched all of this transpire and knew this was his chance. The women walked over to his booth, but instead of dropping everything and giving them a lively welcome, he continued packing up his display. He politely told the ladies he wished they had gotten there earlier because he would have had time to go over his fabulous product. But he had another appointment early the next day and had to get home to prepare. Upon hearing this, the ladies became even more interested. This man didn't need their business. He has customers buying from him all the time. His product must be good. They begged him to take just a moment and go over his presentation for them. The salesman, of course, obliged.

After he made his pitch, the ladies seemed interested. They asked questions and debated on price. The salesperson knew that he just needed to tip them over the fence. He looked at both of them and said, "Look, ladies, this is a great computer. It's going to give you just what you need. But my time is precious, so if you want to buy it—that's great. If not, I am going to have to finish packing up now."

He looked them both dead in the eye and said nothing. The women looked at each other and then back at the salesperson.

"We'll take it," they said.

Never Let Him See You Sweat

As bad as a salesperson needs to make a sale, we cannot show that to the customer. We have to make customers want our product, and that won't happen if they sense we need them to buy it. We know that customers are evaluating our product, and if they perceive us as being anxious for a sale, they will start having second thoughts. They will wonder, *Why is this person so eager for me to buy? Is it because no one else has? Am I the only person who has shown interest? Why is this salesperson so needy?*

If a man perceives you as anxious for a relationship or just generally overly interested in him within the first several dates, he will wonder the same thing. The only way to combat neediness is to act indifferent. Just like the second salesperson, you too have to convey the take-it-or-leave-it attitude. You must have the mentality that if this person doesn't buy it, someone else surely will because your product is just that good. When a customer (or a man) sees that, the product instantly becomes more attractive.

The trick is to keep your indifference at the most crucial times. When the second salesperson saw that the ladies were still undecided, he knew they could have gone either way. He was smart though. Instead of acting out of desperation, he fought back his need for the sale and poured on more indifference. He never let the women see him sweat.

There will be times when you will feel the urge to act out of neediness, too. Things may not be going in your favor, and your natural reaction may be to hold on even tighter, or worse, beg to get your way. But remember, you can never convince someone to want you by saying how much you need them. No matter what, you must keep your indifference. You, too, can never let him see you sweat.

Not Too Hot, Not Too Cold, but Just Right

Terri and Kim were two friends I counseled last summer. They both had trouble keeping men interested. Their relationships never lasted more than a few weeks. The funny thing was they both took the complete opposite approach with men. Terri was afraid that men wouldn't like her if she didn't seem totally interested in them. She told me point-blank, "I'm afraid if I don't give a guy 100 percent of my attention, he will think I'm not interested and then he won't be interested. I feel like I need to show a guy how much I like him because that is what I would want him to do."

On the other hand, Kim always acted completely disinterested in men. She would play hard to get and would often get mad at them for little things in an effort to keep them in pursuit. But the opposite of love is not hate, it's indifference, and her tactics started wearing guys thin. Eventually they grew tired of her cold, hard exterior and believed her to be just bitchy in general.

Kim and Terri didn't realize it but they were both ruining their own chances for a relationship. Terri was too hot, showing too much affection from the very start, and Kim was too cold, acting completely disinterested and snobbish. Instead of sitting at opposite ends of the spectrum, they both needed to move toward the middle.

You want to convey to a man that you like him, yes, but if the relationship doesn't happen, so what? You'll move on and be just fine. That is what indifference truly is. Not too hot, not too cold, just right.

Seeming Indifferent

As I said before, there will be times when it is vitally important to be indifferent. Typically, that moment comes when you are either waiting to hear from a guy or when he seems to be pulling away from you. I remember when I started dating my husband I would almost go crazy waiting to hear from him. After our first date he dropped me off at my apartment and told me he would call me, but he never said when, so I had no idea what time or day to expect his call. He also never texted me with the typical after-the-date follow-up text, which I also was not used to. As I paced around my apartment the next day, I had a momentary lapse in judgment and found myself contemplating texting him first! Thank goodness I didn't. My phone eventually rang that evening, and even though I really wanted to pick up and tell him how much I enjoyed our date and wanted to see him again, I instead sent him straight to voice mail. It was a hard thing to do, but I wanted to seem indifferent. If I picked up right away and gushed about our date, he would have known how excited I was about him, and since we had only been on one date, it was not the time to do that.

I believe that the best way to incorporate just the right amount of indifference is to not answer your phone or immediately return a text for the first several weeks of dating. Whenever you are dating someone new, I advise waiting twenty-four hours  before texting or calling them back. This may sound like a really long time to not respond, but think about how long you waited to hear from the guy in the first place. If you have waited two days to hear from him, is it really so cruel to make him wait a day to hear back from you? If you continue to wait and intermittently return his messages, you will also protect yourself from the dreaded pull-away that some men regularly demonstrate.

April, who is thirty-five, has had trouble with men her whole life. Her biggest problem is that she is super impatient and cannot stand to wait to hear from someone. So when she started dating Drew, a thirty-six-year-old government contractor, I knew that it was very likely that she would scare him away with her neediness within a matter of weeks.

At first things were going well and Drew texted or called April at least every other day. On the days he did not call or text, he would send her an e-mail or a funny forward. Then it happened. Drew skipped a day of contact, and April called me freaking out.

"He always contacts me every other day!" she cried, "but today, nothing. Nothing all day. I have not heard from him in two days now. What should I do?" she whined.

"You shouldn't do anything," I told her. "This is what I've been talking about, April. When something changes and you think a guy might be pulling away, you should not run after him. This is when you really practice indifference," I told her.

"Do nothing? Just wait to hear from him?"

"Yes. Then when you do, do not answer the phone. You need to make him wait a little while to hear back from you now," I pointed out.

"That is so difficult for me, Jess. I just want to call him and make sure we are still okay. I don't know if I can wait to hear from him, let alone wait a day to call him back if I do," she said.

"Well, you can do it your way, April, but your way has not worked well in the past," I reminded her.

April thought about it and decided I was right. Although it was extremely hard for her to do, she waited to hear from Drew. He finally called the next day and she let it go to voice mail. When he didn't hear back from her that night, guess what he did? He called again! He left another message saying he was worried that she was mad at him for not calling earlier. When April called Drew back, she was as sweet as pie, and they picked up right where they left off.

When you learn to add just a little indifference into your dating life, the reward will always outweigh the risk. It may be hard to resist answering a call or quick text, but even if you can hold off replying for a few hours, it will help you to convey a more confident persona. Guys want to date women who like them, yes, but they don't want to date women who they feel need them in order to function.

Playing Your Cards Right

You have to give the impression that you really are indifferent . . . at least for a little while. When you are just getting to know someone, you may find he does things a little differently from how you would do them, or he may live life in a way that doesn't exactly gel with yours. It is not your job to react to these things in the beginning. Instead, you should just observe and learn. Freaking out over small stuff and questioning a man to death is not being indifferent. If he goes out of town, for instance, and doesn't call you, file that away in the back of your mind as a data point about him. He may not be as reliable as you think, and that is something that is good to know. You have to figure out if he is the right type of person for you to be with, and you cannot evaluate that if you immediately attempt to conform him to your way of doing things.

Do not yell and scold him for anything he does in the first couple of months. He's not your boyfriend yet, and you don't have the right to kick and scream anyway. You have to be cool, calm, and relaxed in order to seem indifferent, and to allow him to be who he really is. Anything less than that shows too much emotion too soon. Think of it like playing poker. You may have a full house, but if you let everyone at the table know it, you are going to lose. You need a good poker face. That way you can get what you want and take home the jackpot, or, if necessary, fold your hand and start again.

Don't tell a guy that you are doing any of these things on purpose. Sometimes women get nervous and actually confess the reason they are playing it cool. That's like announcing that you are about to bluff in the middle of a game. Don't tell him what's really going on when you use any of these techniques.

You want him to think it's because you are still on the fence about him and he needs to win you over. You don't want to tell him it's because you read this book. If you tell him you are doing all these things on purpose, with an agenda, he really will think you are playing a game.

Launching Your Relationship

If you only learn one lesson from this book, let this be it. It's by far the most important to understand and utilize. For a relationship to go from casual to serious, both involved people have to feel the same way about each other at exactly the same time. So if you give off the vibe you are ready for a relationship before he does, you will be making a very bad play. Think of it like launching a spaceship where the pilot and the navigator have to turn their keys at precisely the same moment. Because most people don't fall in love at the exact same moment, many relationships fail to launch because one person arrives early to the ship and jams in a key, while the other person is still en route to the launch pad. Don't be that eager person. You will ultimately scare the guy off by showing him how you feel before he does. It may be what you want to do, but I promise you will end up alone waiting on the tarmac. The best thing to do is to remain indifferent—or at least act as if you are. If you feel yourself on the road to the launch pad, pull over into the cell phone waiting area!

The Mirror Theory

Ask any salesperson and they will tell you that 90 percent of communication with their customers is nonverbal. When I would sit down with customers, I'd listen to what they would tell me, but I also paid very close attention to their body language. I have met with customers who have verbally told me that they love my product. However, their body language tells me that they aren't really sold yet. Maybe they have their arms crossed, maybe they won't look me in the eye, maybe it's just the expression on their face. There are so many nonverbal clues that are dead giveaways to what a person is really thinking. It is much more important to read those signs because people often cater to what they say, but it is really hard to fake body language. Body language will always give you the true story.

The Not-So-Cozy Couple

While my friend, Elsa, and I were at dinner one night, I noticed a couple sitting to our right. The girl was a very cute blonde and the guy was a preppy Zac Efron–type. Their body language could not have been more different. He was sitting back with one arm perched on the back of the chair. His other arm rested comfortably in front of him. He seemed distracted and was constantly looking around the room at people nearby. The girl, on the other hand, was fixated on the guy. She was leaning over most of the table to hold his hand. She rubbed his arm lovingly, while he scratched at a spot on his shirt. I turned to Elsa to point them out.

"See that couple over there?" I motioned. "See how the girl is so much more interested in him than he is into her?"

Elsa glanced over. "Wow! She's practically climbing over the table to hold his hand. Meanwhile, he is just relaxing back in his chair, not looking terribly impressed with her."

Just as we were wrapping up the conversation, the guy turned toward us and said, "You girls want to share what you've been saying about us for the last ten minutes?"

My face must have turned beet red. I was totally caught off guard, but worst of all, what was I going to say? "Oh, I was just noticing how your girlfriend is totally in love with you, but you seem to be more interested in the stain on your tie"?

"Oh, um . . . I am writing a book, and I usually observe couples," I blurted out. "I like to guess by their body language what their relationship is like."

The girl sat up in her chair. She hadn't noticed at all that we had been talking about them. She was too busy staring into Zac's dreamy, noncommittal eyes.

"Oh how fun! What did you notice about us?"

"Well . . ." I stammered. "I noticed that you guys have probably been in a relationship for a very long time."

"We have!" she exclaimed. "I just moved here a few months ago from Texas to be with him. It was a surprise."

I could tell by the look on the guy's face, it was more shock than surprise.

"Well, that's great. Long distance is hard. I'm sure he's glad to have you as a roommate now," I said jokingly.

"Actually, we don't live together yet," the girl said, seeming embarrassed. "But I think that's going to change soon. Right, honey?"

The guy sat up and loosened his tie. "Well, uh. I think we need to still talk a little more about that actually."

The girl looked at him as if he had just insulted her mother.

"What do you mean, we need to talk about that? I thought we settled that. I move fifteen hundred miles to be closer to you, and you still want to have distance between us?"

I quickly grabbed the check and paid the bill. Elsa and I couldn't get out of there fast enough. I had just triggered a fight, and it wasn't going to be pretty. Maybe if she had listened to his body language, she would have seen it coming. But it was clear. She wasn't aware of nonverbals. Not his, and not her own.

Some salespeople are so desperate to make a sale that they may as well have a sign posted on their forehead. They never tell the customer how much they need their business, but it's obvious from the look in their eyes or the expression on their face. You, too, can unknowingly communicate to a man that you are longing to find love, or even just uncertain of yourself. A few twirls of your hair or bites of your nails, and the smell of eagerness and insecurity will be palpable. Even though Kristen Stewart made lip biting look cool, try and remember you are not likely to be going out with a vampire anytime soon.

You want to convey confidence and self-assuredness on your dates, and that requires paying close attention to your body language. I know it's not always easy to do. You have so many things to remember while dating that you could go crazy if you think about them all at once. In fact, too much thinking is the very thing that can cause you to forget to pay attention to your body behavior. Luckily for you, there is an easy way to keep your nonverbal communication under tight control.

Years ago, while out with my girlfriends one night, I met a very attractive guy. His name was Kevin, and he was classic tall, dark, and handsome. Just from the look of him, I knew that he could have his pick of women. He asked for my number that night and we set up a date for the following week.

I met Kevin for drinks at a hotel bar in Dupont Circle. We had only discussed having drinks, which was fine with me. I didn't want to be stuck having dinner if the date didn't go well, and I knew he felt the same way. When I walked in and saw him, I was immediately excited. He was a lot cuter than I remembered, and I remembered him being pretty cute. But, because of this, I reminded myself that a lot of other women probably found him attractive, too, so I knew I had to play it cool. I wasn't concerned about saying the right things, but I knew that I had to watch my body language. It was rare for me to be so initially attracted to someone I hardly knew, and I didn't want to blow the date before it even got started.

I remembered an old trick I used during meetings with clients. It's called the Mirror Theory. If I wanted a customer to be completely comfortable, and me not to seem desperate for them to buy, I would mirror their body language. However they were sitting or standing, I would mirror. If they were talking fast or slow, I would mirror. Whatever nonverbals they were giving me, I would reflect the same back.

When Kevin and I were sitting at the bar, he had his whole body turned toward me. I mirrored that and sat with my whole body turned toward him. When he sat back, I sat back. When he leaned in, I leaned in. After sitting at the bar for an hour, he asked me if we could continue our date over dinner.

We walked to a sushi place nearby, and Kevin grabbed my hand. I made a joke about him being a fast mover. He dropped my hand and looked disappointed. I laughed and told him he could hold my hand, I didn't mind. Then I gave him a flirty smile, and he picked up my hand again.

At dinner I continued to use the Mirror Theory. When he was smiling, I was smiling. When he was serious, I was serious. Halfway through our meal, he stopped midsentence and told me something that validated every move I had made up to that point.

"I have to admit, I am a little intimidated by you," he said. "Most of the girls I go out with, I can tell within minutes that they are totally into me. But with you, I can't tell just how much you like me yet. That's odd for me."

"How can you tell when other girls are into you?" I asked.

"Well, they sort of hang on my every word. They giggle a little too much. They think everything I say is funny, even when it's not. They look at me like they are dying for me to kiss them. I don't get any of that from you. I feel like you are smarter than the average bear. Like I said, it is a little intimidating, but I am totally up for the challenge. In fact, I find it extremely refreshing."

Kevin had no clue that all I had been doing that night was mirroring his every move. All he knew was he wanted to see me again.

Mirror, Mirror on the Date

Using the Mirror Theory is a safe way to keep yourself in check throughout your date. It will prevent you from coming on too strong and seeming too interested too soon. It will also prevent you from coming off too cold, which a lot of girls do because they are so afraid of being transparent. Remember, guys want to know that you like them; they just don't want to think you love them. At least not yet. Using Mirror Theory will have your body language just right.

In addition to his body language, you also want to pay attention to a guy's tone of voice and facial expressions. Maybe you didn't tell him how you think he walks on water, but the sound of your voice or look on your face did. Some women think that sounding like Paris Hilton and putting on a "baby voice" is cute and sexy, but the truth is that it's unattractive and could give a guy the impression you aren't that smart. Besides, most of the time people use that voice to talk to children and animals. This is a man, not a Shar-Pei. You want to come off confident, smart, and sophisticated. You don't want to talk like a two-year-old. Some women talk like this on purpose and others don't even realize they are doing it, so try to be conscious of your tone of voice at all times.

Although I'm a firm believer that you are never fully dressed without a smile, some girls overdress for the occasion. On a first date you want to keep a pleasant smile on your face, but you don't have to plaster on a constant grin for a man to know you are having a good time. Laughing at his jokes is always recommended, but be conscious of the fact that you don't want to laugh at everything he says simply because you are nervous. Smile and laugh when he does. Mirror the look on his face. Try not to beam at him as if you are staring into your future and you like what you see. Watch him, mirror his body language, and you will be just fine.

Mirror, Mirror on the Phone

Mirror Theory is something you can use even when you aren't on dates. You can apply it when you are communicating on the phone or over e-mail. Just as we talked about the KISS Principle earlier, you want to make sure you aren't too over-eager off the bat, so use Mirror Theory to clue you in on how and when to respond to a man's e-mails or text messages. If he takes an hour to text you, for instance, wait an hour to respond back. If his e-mails are quick and to the point, mirror him and write back in the same manner. The only time to be careful of mirroring a guy is if he starts coming on too strong. You don't want to mirror everything he does. If he starts blowing up your phone and filling your inbox with texts, that does not give you the green light to do the same. You still have to keep in mind that building a relationship takes time, and if the guy is trying to rush that in the beginning, it does not mean you should just let him. You want him to be calling and texting you more than you are calling or texting him. Don't be afraid to pump the brakes. It will just provide a little more of a challenge, which he will surely enjoy!

Remember, when you start dating someone new, he may not feel the way you do yet, so it's always better to play it cool. By using the Mirror Theory, you are taking interest cues from your date, and you can't show too much interest if you are just mirroring his.

The Jones Effect

When I was nineteen, I was head over heels for my best friend Elliot. He and I worked together promoting various nightclubs. For years I pined away for him while he romanced other women. They came and went, but I remained a constant. Always by his side, always there when he needed me. I thought of myself like his girlfriend; he thought of me like a little sister. I was always careful not to flirt with men around him. I didn't want him to think I was unavailable in case he suddenly decided he was in love and couldn't live without me.

After years of patiently waiting, I decided I'd had enough. My prayers had fallen on deaf ears, and Elliot was never going to come around. As hard as it was to accept, I knew I would have to move on. While Elliot was away on summer break, I met Philip. Philip was a handsome French American who really liked me. Wherever we went, women would comment on my delicious piece of arm candy. And while I certainly had an affinity for Philip, I still harbored feelings for Elliot.

The night Elliot returned from summer vacation, he threw a party at our club. Usually I would show up with girlfriends, but this time I brought Philip with me. As I approached the front door, Elliot greeted me with a huge bear hug. "Hi, gorgeous!" he exclaimed. "How have you been?"

He hadn't yet realized I came with the Lacoste model standing to my right. Suddenly I lost my nerve and wanted to push Philip into the bushes so I wouldn't have to explain him. But before I could find a shrub big enough to hide him, Philip extended his hand.

"Hi, you must be Elliot. I'm Philip."

Elliot went from excitement to confusion. He shook Philip's hand and then looked at me askance.

"Well, seems like you've been busy while I was away," he said.

I didn't know what to say, so I shrugged. Elliot looked at me for a minute and then lifted the velvet rope for Philip and me.

"I'll see you guys inside," he said.

Philip and I settled at a table with some friends. Elliot came over a couple of times to say hello, and each time Philip seemed to take his cue and kiss me. I could tell Elliot was a little weirded-out by the whole thing. Never in the two years that I knew him had he seen me with another guy. I was dying to run after him and scream, "I don't like Philip! I'm sorry! Let's go back to the way it used to be!" But then I remembered: the way it used to be wasn't any better than this. I ordered another drink, wishing I were twenty-one so I could dull the pain with something stronger than a Shirley Temple.

At the end of the night we all stood outside. Philip was tired and wanted to go home. I told him I would catch a ride with someone else since I wanted to go to the after-hours party. As he leaned in to kiss me, I saw Elliot watching from the corner of my eye.

As soon as Philip left, Elliot grabbed me.

"You're staying out?" he asked.

"Yeah, if that's okay?" I said puzzled.

Elliot smiled and took my hand. He yelled to one of his friends that we would meet him at the late-night spot.

Elliot held my hand as we walked to the car, something he had never done before. He opened my door to let me in. I turned to thank him and suddenly before I knew what was even happening, he was kissing me! Elliot and I were kissing! Right there in the parking lot. I couldn't believe it. He pulled backed, looked deep into my eyes, and then said, "You're not really into that guy are you?"

That was the night I learned about the Jones Effect.

What Is the Jones Effect?

The Jones Effect is the highly proven theory that you want what other people have. That is why you will often hear salespeople say, "Everyone is buying one of these. In fact, I sold one to your neighbor yesterday." We know if you think other people are buying, you will want to buy, too. The Jones Effect is so powerful it can take even the most unlikely product and turn it into a bestseller. Remember that old eighties movie *Can't Buy Me Love*? Patrick Dempsey played Ronald Miller, a geeky high school student who mowed lawns and had a crush on the captain of the cheerleaders. He was such a social outcast that he sat in the visiting section at football games. Not only did girls not like him, they didn't even acknowledge his existence.

Then he had a brilliant idea! Ronald, who had always dreamed of being well-liked, paid popular girl Cindy Mancini $1,000 to go out with him in the hopes that it would boost his social standing. Cindy doubted Ronald's popularity plan and scoffed, "Just going out with me is not going to make you popular." To which Ronald replied, "Well, I have a thousand dollars that says it will."

He was right. After one month of pseudodating, Cindy and Ronald annulled their fake relationship and Ronald became the hottest item on the school's menu. Every girl wanted to date the guy who had gone from geek to chic. Ronald was a social leper until Cindy came along. But with her approval, the entire student body had a sudden change of heart.

Why is the Jones Effect so effective in convincing people they like something? Why do we need social proof that others feel the way we do? Right or wrong, it's human nature to believe if someone else likes what we like, it validates it as being good.

Most of my friends have never heard of the Jones Effect, and if they have, they don't know how to use it. We often don't want the guy we like to think we're into (or going out with) someone else because we think that he may get discouraged and give up on us. But that is honestly a misconception. Guys who are genuinely interested in you won't give up without trying first, and they won't see you as liking someone else (although it's not always a bad thing to make them worry that you might). All a guy sees is someone else wanting you, and that is a good thing. Other men should want you. You are a desirable woman who men would kill to be with, and he needs to know that. Seeing you talk to another man will not deter him from pursuing you. On the contrary, it will only fuel the fire if you do it right.

Keep Him Jonesing

When you begin dating someone, it's perfectly fine for him to think you are out with other men. It's okay to talk about your male friends, because he should know that they exist. You are too cute and funny to not have any men in your life. Don't feel the need to always explain where you are and who you are with. You want him to question if you have another date. If he says something to you about it, you can always come back with, "I didn't realize we were only dating each other exclusively. I'm sorry, should we talk about it?"

You should chat to and be friendly with men around you, even if it's just the waiter or doorman. As the relationship progresses, you can tone it down, but you don't want to let it go completely. Men are competitive by nature, and they like feeling as if they have a woman that other men want.

Jones Effect = Attractive

Think about how many times you have been affected by the Jones Effect. When you find out a guy has a girlfriend or see a ring on his finger, don't you automatically find him slightly more attractive? Of course you do—because someone else has him. He is desirable to at least one other person. Don't go stealing someone else's boyfriend now that I've pointed that out. All I am saying is that if you have absolutely no one wanting you, what does that say? Don't hide the fact that you have guy friends. You don't have to ignore other guys at a party. Don't be afraid to let him see you interact or talk with members of the opposite sex. Unless he's very insecure, it will not prevent him from liking you. Don't be obvious about it, but don't hide it either.

But Be Warned . . .

Now a word of caution: the Jones Effect must be used with kid gloves. You don't want to overdo it. There are women who go overboard with their use of the Jones Effect. I have a friend who flirts like crazy with other guys when she's out with her boyfriend. She loves to make him jealous. Every time they go out together, she starts flirting with the waiter, the bartender, the man in line for the restroom, and anyone else she comes in contact with. She becomes very touchy-feely with them too. I've seen her sit on a random guy's lap in an effort to get a rise out of her boyfriend. He knows what she is doing and it creates a lot of drama between them. That's not using the Jones Effect; that's abusing it.

There is a difference between being friendly with guys and overtly flirting with them. You don't want to give men the wrong idea or the impression that you are interested in them when you are not, especially if you are on a date with someone else. There is a fine line here. If you are unsure of using this technique with guys, incorporate it with women, too. If you make new female friends as well as male ones, you will just be seen as friendly to everyone.

Don't drop too many boy names when it comes to the Jones Effect either. If you are always talking about your friend Mike who likes you, or your coworker Bob who calls you too much, you will be perceived as boastful and arrogant. Used wisely, the Jones Effect can be a good tool. Used foolishly, however, it can be deadly.

CHAPTER SIX

keeping him interested

Hold Back Your Bullets

I'll never forget the first woman to ever cry in my office. Her name was Amelia. She was a tiny blonde with a big personality. Her blue eyes, which were usually filled with excitement and enthusiasm, were now flooded with tears and runny mascara. As she sat in front of me trying to find her words, I remember thinking she looked more like a woman who had just lost her boyfriend instead of a sale.

But that's why she was sobbing so profusely. She had been pounding the pavement for weeks, trying to find new customers. Ten different business owners had invited her to sit down and give them her pitch about switching phone carriers, but as time progressed she was unable to close any of them.

"I just don't understand it," she cried. "None of the other reps had as many deals in their funnel. Yet, they were able to close at least two or three people. I couldn't close anyone. I feel so stupid. I don't think I can work here anymore."

Although she was being a bit dramatic, she was right. Having ten deals in her funnel was unusual. Most of the other reps didn't have nearly that good of a prospecting rate. Amelia was able to get customers interested, but somewhere in the course of the sale, she was losing them. She knew it, and that's why she felt so bad.

"Hey, you have gotten through the toughest part. Finding the business and getting the person interested to hear what you have to say is what takes the most effort. You just need to figure out what you are doing that is losing the customers' interest. Tell me exactly what happened with each person and we'll figure it out together," I said.

Though her sniffles, Amelia recounted the last few weeks for me. As I listened to her story I began to realize her problem. Amelia started off strong when she first sat down with a potential buyer. She always smiled and broke the ice before diving into her pitch. However, halfway through her presentation, she became nervous that the client wasn't warming up to her offer and she started throwing out incentives to entice them more. She gave them free pens, offered to lower their long-distance rate with no obligation, and even told them about the thirty-day free trial—something I had taught the reps to hold back on and use only to tip a customer over the fence. Because Amelia was so afraid that the customer would lose interest, she told them about all the perks right up front instead of pacing the conversation and dishing them out accordingly.

"Amelia," I said. "Has anyone told you about the Bullet Theory?"

"Um . . . no," she replied.

"Think of all the perks of our contract as bullets. Free long-distance is a bullet. The thirty-day trial is a bullet. Even these silly little pens are bullets. You only have a handful to use in order to keep your customers interested. The sales process can take a long time, and if you throw all of them out right away, you are going to be left with no ammunition. So you want to divvy out your bullets little by little when they are really needed. You threw out all your bullets on the first meeting, so by the second or third visit, your customers started to lose interest, and you had nothing left to entice them with."

Amelia realized what she was doing wrong. She tried to fix it, but she was never able to hold back her bullets. She was too fearful that the customer would lose interest right away. She continued to throw out her bullets too soon and ultimately she had to find another job.

Single women sometimes have the same problem as Amelia.

They throw out all their bullets right away, too. In dating, however, bullets are a woman's valuables, such as kissing, making out, and the biggest bullet of all, sex. Some women think if they don't throw out these bullets right away, a guy actually won't like them. But, as I explained to Amelia, keeping your bullets is the predominant way to keep someone's interest.

Emptying Your Gun

Sylvia was a thirty-five-year-old attorney. She was attractive and successful, but she hadn't had a serious relationship in years.

"Tell me about the last two guys you were interested in," I said to her.

"Well, first there was Josh. I met Josh at a Halloween party given by a friend of mine. I had seen him around, but we had never really talked before. We struck up a conversation that lasted most of the night. He asked for my number and we went out that weekend."

"Okay, so how did the first date go?"

"It went alright. He came over and we were going to go out to dinner but instead we ordered in and watched a movie. Well, we didn't really watch the movie. But I still had a good time."

"So you guys made out all night?"

"Yeah, you could say that," she laughed.

"Did you have sex?" I asked.

"No, but we came very close a couple of times."

"Okay, what happened after that night?"

"We went out again. We went to a party and then back to his place . . . and uh, that time we had sex," she said with an embarrassed laugh.

"Hmmm, okay. So you went on two dates before becoming intimate?"

"Yeah. We saw each other for about two weeks after that and everything was fine. Then he had to go out of town for work. I didn't hear from him when he came back, so I called him. He didn't pick up, so I left a message on his machine. I don't know what happened, but that was two weeks ago now, and he still hasn't returned my call."

"So you never heard from him again?" I said.

"No."

I wanted to tell Sylvia what she did wrong in that situation, but I wanted to see if she was a habitual offender, so I asked her to tell me about the second guy, too.

"Last weekend I went to this concert in the park by my house and I saw this really hot guy. I smiled at him, and he came right over. We hung out the rest of the night and had a blast. He was definitely one of the coolest guys I have met in a long time. Anyway, I must have been drinking more than I should have because we ended up back at my place. Anyway, long story short, we did not have sex but we did spend hours making out. Finally we both fell asleep."

"So what happened the next day? Did you have breakfast together? Or did he leave right when you guys woke up?" I asked. Sylvia's eyes dropped to her feet. "When I woke up, he was gone. He didn't leave a note or a number."

It was clear. She was a habitual offender. The crime: misuse of a firearm.

I had to explain the Bullet Theory to Sylvia. She was great at meeting guys and getting them interested, but she was losing them because she was throwing out all her bullets on the first couple of dates. She spent too much time with them (missing the Height of Impulse) and became intimate with them way too soon. Even though she didn't have sex with the second guy, the fact that she almost did told him that all it would take would be one more date.

"Sylvia, your affection and your body are all precious things. You don't even really know these guys and you are giving yourself away within the first few dates. The second guy didn't even take you out to dinner and you almost slept with him. You have to hold your bullets back or men will lose interest in you."

"Okay, maybe I screwed up with Josh, but I didn't sleep with the concert guy," she interjected. "Isn't that what's really the most important thing here? You aren't supposed to have sex on the first date, and I did not do that."

"No, you didn't. But believe me, he knew that it wasn't going to be long before you gave in," I told her. "Look, the concert guy didn't call you because based on how you acted the first night, he knew he was going to get you into bed quickly. He either didn't want to sleep with a girl that he assumed had been around the block, or he figured the reward of sleeping with you wasn't worth the risk of you becoming emotionally attached. There aren't a lot of girls who sleep with men and don't want something more from them. So most guys, believe it or not, would rather turn down sex than do it and have to spend weeks shaking an emotionally attached girl off their tail."

Sylvia looked dumbfounded. How was all this so obvious to me and news to her?

Unfortunately, most girls suffer the same consequences of throwing out all their bullets. In Sylvia's case, she had wanted someone to like her so badly that she jumped all over any guy who showed interest. She needed to learn to keep her gun locked and loaded in order to keep her dates coming back for more.

Building Anticipation

When I was a kid, my favorite time of year was right before Christmas. My parents would put up a big tree and my sister and I would decorate it with dozens of colorful ornaments. We'd sing carols and make cookies. All of our family would visit, and each would bring a present that we were instructed to put under the tree. As the days passed and Christmas neared, the presents began to pile up. My sister and I would shake and rattle them with glee, wondering what was inside. We begged our mother to let us open just one, but she firmly told us no. We had to wait until Christmas day.

On Christmas Eve we couldn't sleep. We tossed and turned in our beds, wishing it was morning so we could run downstairs and tear into our presents. Then at 7:00 AM we'd burst into our parents' room, jumping on the bed, pleading with them to wake up and let Christmas day begin. We'd open our gifts and spend days under the tree playing. I remember taking all my presents to bed and sleeping with them for a week.

That is how I remember the holidays. I can't recall any of the presents I received, but I do remember the wonderfully agonizing feeling of anticipation. It went on for weeks, and it filled our house with excitement. It wasn't the presents that made it so thrilling; it was the waiting to open them that did it.

You have to think of yourself as a present under the tree. You want a guy to be so anxious and eager to open you up, he can hardly stand it. You want to build anticipation within him, and you cannot do it if you throw out your bullets right away. Imagine if my mother gave in every time my sister and I begged to open a gift before Christmas. Then the anticipation would only last for moments instead of for weeks. The excitement would never build, and we'd not cherish the gifts as much. If you meet a guy, and within a few dates (or worse, a few hours) he gets what he wants from you, he won't cherish you either.

There is a direct correlation between waiting for something and cherishing it once you have it. The longer you wait, the more you want it, and the happier you are when you get it. Knowing this basic principle, you should understand why it is in your best interest to hold back your bullets. Not just the sex bullet—all of them. The longer a guy waits, the better.

Do Bullets Expire?

But eventually you have to throw out all your bullets, right? Isn't there a point at which a guy will lose interest if things aren't progressing physically? Don't bullets have an expiration date? The answer is no. They aren't like a carton of milk. Bullets don't go bad. When you hold back your bullets, you are conveying the message that you really respect yourself. When you throw them out right away, you are saying that you don't. Respect is contagious, just like confidence. If you respect yourself, others will respect you. If you don't respect yourself, don't expect anyone else to either. If a guy pressures you, especially for sex, then you really need to question what his motive is for seeing you. If he tells you that sex is really important to him and he cannot see you anymore if you two aren't having it, then dump him. He's being selfish and he's only after one thing.

Personally, I rarely kissed on a first date. Sometimes, I didn't even kiss on the second or third. Sounds crazy, right? But it was holding back this bullet that put me in a whole other category from other women. By holding back the kissing bullet, I was subsequently holding back several other bullets, too. That one bullet helped me hold back a lot of the other ones.

When I told Sylvia this she looked at me like I was out of my mind. She couldn't hold back for one hour, let alone one full date.

"Doesn't the guy think you are weird? Doesn't he assume you aren't interested? Won't he think I'm boring or a prude?" she asked.

"No. I was still flirty. I hugged. I kissed on the cheek, and I smiled. If the guy went in for a real kiss, I would just say, 'I'm sorry, I'm just not ready to kiss you yet.' If he asked when I would be ready to kiss him, I told him that I really didn't know. I liked to build up the desire to kiss someone. It may take one date, it may take four. But the honest truth is, most guys never even asked why I was not kissing them. They just accepted it and grew even more excited for it to happen."

Sylvia was amazed. "I feel like I have to kiss them or they will lose interest and move on to someone else."

"And that is the exact opposite of what will happen," I told her.

A good salesperson knows how to use her bullets. If you throw them out too soon, you can jeopardize the sale. Likewise, if you throw out yours too soon, you can jeopardize your relationship. You have to keep your gun loaded at all times, even if you are dying to fire it off. I know there will also be times that your hormones will be raging and holding back won't be easy. But it is what is necessary! If you don't want a long-term relationship with a guy, go ahead and sleep with him after two dates. Just understand that men don't respect or seriously date women they have sex with so soon. He may stick around a little while if you are lucky, but even if you get a relationship out of him, I guarantee it won't be the one you want. In the back of his head he will always think you sleep around. It won't matter if you tell him that you don't typically do that sort of thing and he's the only one you have ever done this with. What you say is always canceled out by what you do.

Keep Your Bullets, Keep Your Sanity

Last year I received an e-mail from a girl named Jamie. She was twenty-five years old and very tired of casually hooking up. She told me that she had dated almost every man in the New York City area, and she was worried there would soon be no one left! Jamie had no problem meeting men; she was very attractive and met them everywhere. The trouble was that after two or three months of dating, things quickly went south and the relationship fell apart. She desperately wanted to stop this pattern, because she had just started dating someone new, and according to her calculations, the relationship was about to tank any day now. Within ten minutes of our conversation, I uncovered the root cause of Jamie's problem. Here is just a little bit of our conversation:

Me: What happens with these guys at the two- to three-month marker?

Jamie: I get really antsy, I guess. I start to worry that things are not going in the right direction because we have not discussed the relationship yet.

Me: And when you worry, what do you do?

Jamie: I typically put pressure on the guy. I may text him more or ask him what's going on with us. I think I may get a little crazy. I sometimes drive by their house at night to make sure they are home.

Me: And when you get a little crazy, they back off completely.

Jamie: Correct.

Me: So what we have to do is get you to not worry so that you don't go crazy.

Jamie: That sounds good.

Me: When do you usually first have sex with someone?

Jamie: Um, this is going to sound bad, but I usually sleep with them by the third date.

Me: That's your problem then. You are having noncommittal sex with men for two or three months without knowing how they feel about you. That's enough to make anyone crazy. Of course you get nervous. You are giving yourself completely to someone who you aren't even sure is going to call you the next day. If you stop having sex so fast and just date for a few months first, you will be able to combat all this crazy behavior.

Jamie: That's it? All I do is put off sex and the pattern of losing them after two to three months will stop?

Me: Yes, it will. The worry you are having comes from the fear that the man you just slept with won't contact you again. It is devastating to have someone be intimate with you one day and then toss you aside the next. You are so afraid that is going to happen, you start to panic. Then you pressure the guy in order to ease your fear. If you just eliminate the sex from your dates, the worry and the crazy will subside.

So Jamie did just that. The guy she was currently dating did fade away as suspected, but with the very next relationship, she broke the three-month curse. She held back her big bullet for three months and she and the guy dated for almost a year.

When you have sex after only a few dates, you are giving the most important part of yourself to a man you hardly know, and with whom you have no established relationship. Of course you will worry if he will call! Of course you will go crazy if you don't hear from him! You want to trust him, but you can't because you don't know him. Think about this: Would you lend a thousand dollars to a man you had only been on three dates with? Could you trust he would pay you back? If you can't say with 100 percent certainty that he would, then you should not be sleeping with him either.

So when is it appropriate to throw out your bullets? Exactly how long should you wait? There isn't a set timeline. It really depends on how you feel about the relationship. You have to feel comfortable with it as it is and be able to trust that the guy is on the same page as you. Don't think that if you have sex with someone, you will get closer to him and thus get him even more interested. That will not happen. If he's only moderately interested in you now, sex is not going to fuel his "commitment" fire. There are many things you will learn in this book that will help you build interest, but sex is not going to be one of them. Get to know the guy by dating him and not having sex. Until he calls you his girlfriend for at least a few months, that bullet should remain comfortably in its chamber. Once you are in a committed relationship and things are going well, you can enjoy worry-free, passionate lovemaking every day of the week.

Don't Cut to the Close

After dating a workaholic named P.J. for almost a year, my very good friend Isabel realized that he was never going to want to get married or have children. She was angry for wasting so much of her time on him and now had to start all over again. So when she started dating Harrison, she did not want to squander one second of her time if he didn't want to get married and start a family either. After they had been dating a few weeks, she decided to casually ask him one night if he saw marriage and children in his future. Harrison said he definitely wanted to get married and have kids someday. Of course, upon hearing this, Isabel was delighted. She told him she felt that being a mother was her calling in life and couldn't wait to settle down and start a family with someone. She was glad that she and Harrison had the same goals and felt at ease that she was now dating someone who wanted to be married and have children, too.

I spoke to Isabel shortly after she had this discussion with Harrison. She said it was so nice to finally find someone who was on her level and wanted the same things. She thought Harrison was a good candidate and could see them having a very bright future.

Unfortunately, their relationship did not last long after that conversation. Harrison told her a few weeks later that he just didn't have time for a serious relationship. He told her he thought she was a great person but couldn't commit at this point in his life. Isabel was completely dumbfounded. How could he tell her one minute that he wanted a family and the next minute tell her he didn't even want to commit to being a boyfriend?

Unfortunately, Isabel had made a classic mistake. She had tried to cut to the close.

A lot of my clients and friends complain about the same thing. If they are in their twenties I hear, "I want a boyfriend." If they are in their thirties I hear, "I want to get married." Getting involved in a serious relationship seems to always be in the forefront of their minds. Never do they say, "I want to meet someone who seems right for me, date him, and see if we are compatible." No, when they meet a guy their brain goes straight to relationship mode. Forget casually dating him. They want to find the fastest way to lock him into a commitment.

Even though you may be worried about wasting your time with someone who doesn't want to get married, it doesn't mean you can forgo the dating cycle and ask certain closing questions. You may want to know a man's intentions right away or feel the need to tell him yours, but doing so will only hurt your chances for a future together. I know it may be torture for you to date someone and not know where the relationship is headed, but you have to remember that dating itself is

a wait-and-see period. So unfortunately, you are going to have to spend a little time waiting and seeing if things will work out.

A man can't tell you his intentions right away, because frankly, he doesn't know what they are yet. If you cut to the close and discuss your future relationship goals, you are basically pressuring him to make a decision about something he knows nothing about. You are telling him, "Hey, buddy, don't even think about taking me out again unless you think you want to marry me." Asking a guy whether he wants to get married on the first few dates would be like me meeting a client for the very first time and trying to close him right after introducing myself. Can you imagine if I sat down with a new customer and said, "Hi, my name is Jess, and I am looking to sell this product. But before I even waste my time building a relationship with you, I need to know if you are ever going to buy it. If you don't think you are going to purchase it sometime in the near future, I won't waste my breath. So tell me right now, are you going to buy it or not?"

I would have never sold anything that way. How would a new customer know if they are going to buy my product? They don't know anything about it yet. Just like in dating, you can't go out with a guy on a first date and say you are looking to get married, have kids, buy a house, and call it a day. It will not speed up the dating process for you. In fact, it will bring it to a screeching halt.

Isabel thought because she so casually asked Harrison about marriage and didn't say she wanted to specifically marry him, bringing up the subject would not be a big deal. She could not have been more wrong. Don't ever announce that your next goal in life is to get married and have children. That kind of talk is meant for people who are already involved in a serious relationship. If you bring up the marriage topic with a man you have just started seeing, he is going to think you are trying to marry him. When a guy hears you want a serious relationship of any kind, it doesn't matter if you don't say with whom—he's going to assume you mean him. He's the one sitting across the table from you. He's the one you're dating. Who else could you be talking about?

If you're interested in someone and want to know if marriage is high on his priority list, backing him into a corner with a direct question is not the right way to find out. It's too scary, and it turns guys off. How would you feel if a guy told you what he really wanted on a first date? I imagine it would sound something like, "You know, I just really want to have sex sometime soon. If a woman isn't seriously interested in sex, then I really don't want to waste my time. Can you see yourself doing it in the next few days, weeks, or months from now? I am only interested in dating women who are going to want to have sex in the very near future."

Now, tell me that's a turn-on for you, and if so, you can keep on having your early marriage talks.

Creating Skepticism

Back when I was a sales trainer, I was asked to ride in the field one day with a brand-new sales rep who was having difficulty closing deals. Joe was a former football player who injured himself and was now looking for another career. He told me he wanted to get into sales because he wanted to control his income and get paid what he was worth. Unfortunately, so far his worth was only about thirty-five bucks.

"I don't know what it is, Jess. Maybe I am just not cut out for this. People don't want to buy from me. I think they are intimidated by me."

"Well, Joe, that's why I'm here," I said. "I'm just going to listen today and see if I can determine what you may need to do differently. Usually it's just a matter of tweaking your game. Don't throw in the towel yet."

We walked into a law office, and I let Joe take the reins. Behind the front desk two ladies were chatting away, getting little work done. Perfect, I thought. I knew they were sociable people, and they weren't busy at the moment. Joe kicked off his pitch.

"Hi, how are you doing today, ladies? My name is Joe, and yes, I am a sales rep. But don't worry; I'm not going to sell you something you don't need. I promise you're going to love it. I'm here on behalf of your local phone carrier. We have some new rates, and for only twenty-nine ninety-nine a month, you can get our deluxe package. Do you have a current phone bill I could look at and show you what I'm talking about?"

At that point I couldn't watch the *Titanic* sink. I walked out of the business, knowing Joe would be right behind me. Seconds later the door flew open and Joe stormed out. "That's it. I quit. They wouldn't even let me see a phone bill. I couldn't even get through my pitch. How is it that everyone else can sign up three to four people a day and I haven't signed up one person this week?"

"Joe," I said, "the answer is very simple. It's not that you're intimidating, or that you just aren't cut out for this. You just turned them off before you even got started. The first thing you said in there was 'Hi, I'm a salesperson, and for only twenty-nine ninety-nine, I can sell you this.' Joe, people are automatically skeptical of someone trying to sell them something they don't need, and the first thing you did was announce that you were selling something! Then you told them the price before even getting them interested or explaining the product. You created skepticism, which caused them to put up a wall in defense. You have to get people excited first, and then you can tell them how much the service costs. It doesn't work the other way around."

"But, Jess, don't they already know I'm a salesperson when I walk in the door? And twenty-nine ninety-nine is a good deal. I am just trying to cut to the chase and get down to business. Besides, I say it very casually so they don't feel pressured."

"And how has that been working for you?" I asked.

Price Before Product?

You never want to tell a customer up front that you are about to sell them something, and you never tell them the price in the beginning of a conversation. Price is to be discussed at the end of the sales cycle, after the customer has seen the product and understands its worth. Women who talk marriage too soon are breaking that same rule and making the close much more difficult for themselves. You can't talk about marriage until a guy knows your product—you—and understands the value of it.

People are always a little skeptical that a salesperson is only interested in making money off them. However, once we gain their trust, they will ultimately be fine with buying from us. Women are in the same boat. There are lots of men out there who are known to be skeptical of women. They are skeptical that we are just out to land a husband to take care of us. Your job is to prove them wrong. You aren't looking to get married; you are looking for someone with whom you're compatible. Will it lead to marriage? Hopefully. But the best thing to do is not talk about these thoughts. Not in the beginning anyway. You want to reduce skepticism, not create more.

I told Joe not to announce that he was a salesperson and to wait until the close to discuss the price. I told him to walk in and start out with something light and fun. There is no need to restate the obvious. Yes, he is a salesperson, but the customer doesn't need to be reminded of that.

Joe went to the next business. Instead of walking in and giving his usual pitch, he smiled at the lady at the front desk and
broke the ice first. They chatted for a bit, he made a couple of
jokes, and a few minutes later she was rummaging through her
desk looking for an old phone bill. After that, he had no problem closing the deal.

Qualifying the Guy

Although you can't ask someone up front if they would
be willing to buy from you, there are ways to figure out if a
customer is likely to make a purchase. As I mentioned earlier,
there are people who will fake interest in a salesperson just to
be courteous, so you learn quickly how to gauge who is worth
building a relationship with and who is more likely to waste
your time.

When I was a rookie selling medical equipment, I had a very
large territory. It stretched over three states and took six hours
to drive from one end to the other. I remember one day getting
a call from my farthest hospital. They wanted some information about my product and asked when I'd be back in the area.
I was so excited that someone was actually interested and calling me (not the other way around) that I jumped in the car and
drove six hours to talk with them. When I got there and sat
down to talk with the man who had called, I quickly realized
he had no authority to make a hospital purchase and that the
hospital itself didn't even have money in their budget to buy

that year! I had wasted my entire day driving across county lines to meet with someone who was interested in what I had, but wasn't able to make a deal with me.

I could have spared myself the long car ride if I had simply qualified my buyer before trekking out to see him. I was new at the time, though, and I didn't know to ask certain questions to determine if someone was not only willing but also able to buy. Had I inquired on the phone about the hospital budget and who would be making the final decision, I could have saved myself a little disappointment, as well as a whole tankful of gas.

When you start dating someone new, you may not be able to ask their intentions to commit right away, but you can certainly qualify them ahead of time so that you don't end up dating someone who isn't likely to settle down. There are some men who would rather stay single, and you don't want to invest time and energy into the kind who do. Ask about a man's lifestyle. Is he still living the single life and partying until the wee hours of the morning? If he treasures his freedom and routinely likes to get high or drunk with his friends, he is probably not in a place to make a real commitment to you even if he says he is ready. Inquire about his past relationships as well. Has he ever come close to marriage? Why or why not? If a guy seems to be an eternal bachelor, don't sign up to be another notch in his belt. You want to be with someone who dates women seriously and speaks respectfully of them, even after the breakup. Leave the players playing!

You can also determine a lot about a man by observing what is most important to him. Is it his family and his 401k, or is it his band and his favorite pair of jeans? Of course, there is nothing wrong with someone who dresses well and is musically inclined, but if a guy is twenty-eight and still living in his mother's garage while waiting for his big break, you may want to find someone who is planning for a different kind of future.

Undoubtedly, you will end up going out with a few men who claim they want to marry and start a family on the very first date. By date two they are asking you where you would want the wedding, and by date three they are playfully asking what you guys might name your kids. Be wary of these men! They are looking for sex and trying to cut to the close with you. They know exactly what to say to get you into bed as fast as possible. Knowing how much some women crave commitment, they dangle that carrot right in their faces, priming them for some sex without strings attached. If a guy tells you he thinks you could be The One after only a couple of dates, you really should question his character. He's either a smooth talker with a shady agenda, or, eloquently put, he's a dum-dum who is just desperate.

Again, dating is a getting-to-know-you stage, so in the beginning that is what you should be doing. Get to know the guy so you can assess if he is a good candidate for a serious relationship. Don't ignore red flags. If you sense he has a terrible temper or can't control his urge to drink, move on. If he seems happy playing the field and comes off as flaky as a bowl of Special K, keep walking. These are not attributes that make someone a good boyfriend or husband. You don't want to waste your time with an unqualified candidate, so be sure to really ask your dates questions about themselves and make good decisions based on the information you get.

You may not be able to cut to the close with someone you like, but you can quickly and easily figure out if they are the type to commit or not. If they are, then it will be within your power to keep them interested until you can determine if you are a good match. If they are not the type, however, there is really nothing you can do to change that and it is better to move on and find someone with more like-minded values.

Don't Sweeten the Deal

A new emergency room was being built in the tiny town of Summersville, West Virginia. I had been visiting the facility for months, and finally they were ready to evaluate my equipment. I brought in a brand-new cardiac monitor for the nurses to use for a few weeks, hoping that they would fall in love with it and realize they couldn't live without it. As I was setting up the equipment, I noticed that all the nurses were gathered around a table in the back of the room. I walked over to see what the commotion was about and saw two huge boxes with the words Cheesecake Factory written on top. Suddenly I felt a pang of nervousness. There wasn't a Cheesecake Factory within fifty miles. It could only mean one thing. I quickly scanned the room, looking for what I feared. Suddenly I saw it, there in the corner: an eighteen-inch flat-panel Philips monitor. My competition had beaten me here . . . and they had brought cheesecake.

The topic of conversation that day was not about which monitor the staff liked better. It was about the yummy dessert the oh-so-thoughtful Philips rep had brought them. In a town where a fancy dinner was a night out at Applebee's, the cake from the dessert mecca had the tiny country hospital talking. I was screwed, I thought. My company didn't allow gifts of any sort. I was going to have to do my best to sell the nurses without the help of sugar.

I followed up a week later with the facility. I knew they were going to be deciding soon on which vendor to go with, so I would really have to do my best to convince them they wanted me. I entered the usually busy ER and found only one nurse at the front desk. I was about to ask her if everyone had called in sick when I saw an empty box of Krispy Kremes sitting on the table. As I glanced over to the snack room, I saw all the nurses smiling, laughing, and eating doughnuts.

For the next few weeks I continued to fight a losing battle. The Philips rep was constantly invited back to meet with other staff members, while I had to fight just to get a twenty-minute appointment. On every visit, at least one staff member referenced the doughnuts. One nurse even declared in my presence that she "loved when the Philips rep came to visit!" I got back to my hotel room the last night I was in town and logged on to my e-mail. I was going to have to tell my boss that it wasn't looking good. But just as I signed in, I noticed I had an e-mail from the hospital's director of nursing. She wanted me to come back tomorrow at 7:30 AM to talk. I was curious as to what this meant. I set my alarm and went to bed wondering.

The next day I was at the hospital right on time. I walked into the director's office, and she saw me right away.

"Hi, Jess. Thanks for coming back on such short notice. We have been dragging our feet on buying our new monitors, but we had a meeting late last night and all the nurses agreed that your monitor is the one we want."

"Oh!" I said, a bit too surprised. "That's fantastic."

The director laughed. "You seem surprised."

A bit embarrassed, I felt the need to come clean. "Well, after the Philips rep had brought so many treats for the staff, I was a little worried. They seem to really like the cheesecake and doughnuts," I confessed.

"Oh, they did. They talked about it more than the monitors," she admitted. "But it didn't make us like his monitor. If anything, it actually had the reverse effect. We wondered why he didn't talk about the monitor like you did. All he did was bring us food. Every time we saw him, he had something else to give us. It was almost as if he needed to persuade us with dessert because his product wasn't as good as yours."

I shook my head in agreement. "Yes, I was thinking the same thing. That's why I didn't bring any cake myself."

I think she knew I was lying.

That was the day I learned you don't have to sweeten the deal. You can't hide your product behind gifts and favors, hoping that will win a customer over. The Philips rep was hoping to do that, but in the end, he didn't earn the staff's trust and respect; he was merely used for his Krispy Kremes and cheesecake connections.

Some women believe the way to a man's heart is through his stomach, his laundry, and other tokens of appreciation. But gifts and favors will not make a man like you. In fact, excessive giving with the intention of winning a man's approval will only cheapen you and make it seem like your product is not good enough to stand on its own.

When my client Rhianne started seeing Tom, a real estate agent, she immediately went into her normal routine. They had their first date at a wine bar in D.C., and Rhianne insisted on treating Tom to ice cream afterward. They walked around the city chatting and ended the date around midnight. Rhianne told me she had never had such a wonderful first date and confided in me that she thought she had found someone really special.

Rhianne expected Tom to call the next day, so when he didn't, she grew anxious. When he finally did call two days later, she was so relieved she wanted to do something nice for him. When he asked if he could take her to his favorite Thai restaurant, she told him she had two tickets to the Nationals game and wanted to treat him instead. Tom, naturally, did not say no.

For the next few weeks, Rhianne continued on this track. She would do little things at first, like take Tom's dog for a walk before work or tidy his house if it got messy. Sometimes she would surprise Tom by stocking his fridge with healthy food or buying him a new shirt when she went out shopping. As a few more weeks passed, the favors and gifts got more extravagant. She paid for his car to get detailed, cleaned and organized his garage, and when Tom's fifty-inch flat-screen broke, she bought him a new one.

Tom reciprocated for a while at first, but as they continued to date, he began to do less and less as Rhianne continued to give more and more.

After dating for a year, Tom and Rhianne's relationship became completely imbalanced. Tom did whatever he wanted, whenever he wanted with little regard for how Rhianne felt. He often left her with a list of things to do while he went out with his friends, and rarely thanked her for anything she did for him. I tried to make Rhianne see that she had helped Tom become a very selfish person, and that without a radical change on her part, the relationship was going to get worse.

But just as Rhianne began contemplating leaving Tom, something unexpected happened. He proposed. Rhianne was ecstatic and truly believed that it meant he loved her and would work on improving himself. After two years together, they got married by a justice of the peace. It was not the ceremony she wanted, but Rhianne told herself that the marriage was more important than the wedding.

I wish this story had a happy ending, but, unfortunately, it is a cautionary tale. After being married for a year, Rhianne became pregnant with a baby girl. On the day after she gave birth to their daughter, she found out that Tom had been seeing another woman. She was, of course, devastated. They are now going through divorce proceedings.

The Danger of Giving Too Much

Rhianne mistakenly thought that by giving Tom anything he asked for (and even some things that he didn't), she would have a happy marriage. It was her constant sacrifice, however, that ultimately ruined them. The truth is, if you are going to bend over backward for a guy and continue to always give out of fear he won't love you otherwise, then you are just asking for him to take, take, take. One day you will wake up and realize that you are treated more like a personal assistant than a girlfriend or wife. You will find yourself running all the errands and doing all the dirty work while he kicks back on the couch after his long workday. After a period of time, your relationship will slowly deteriorate, and you will most likely end up back where you started—single. Rhianne's story may be worst-case scenario but nonetheless you can and will ruin a healthy relationship if you constantly feel the need to "sweeten the deal" of being with you. A relationship must have balance to be successful, so if one of you is doing more for the other, you are actually putting yourselves in jeopardy. Excessive gifts and favors won't make a man love you. Remember, a great product doesn't need extra incentives; it can stand confidently on its own.

People Pleasers

Many women consider themselves people pleasers. They enjoy doing nice things for the ones they love, and they don't want to hold back when they are involved with a man. When you first begin seeing someone, however, you have to realize that you are not in a loving relationship just yet. You are merely in the getting-to-know-you phase. If you overgive to a man you've only been dating for a couple of months, you are setting up the relationship for failure. As it continues it will grow into an uneven partnership, so save the pleasing for later, when you've established a commitment and you are getting reciprocity from the guy. When you are married you absolutely can and should put your spouse first, but you aren't married yet—I know, because you wouldn't be reading this book if you were!

Men want to pursue women. It is in their nature. Don't take that away from them by showering them with love, affection, TVs, or other merchandise. Until you are safely and securely in a commitment, save all the giving for your current friends and family.

The bottom line: If you find yourself always aiming to please a guy because you want him to like you, you really need to look at the deeper issue here. You aren't totally sold on your own product yet. Don't even think about the close. You need to go back to the beginning of this book and start over.

CHAPTER SEVEN

closing the deal

Never Assume

After two years in real estate, my mom was about to close the biggest deal in her career. She had been working on selling a million-dollar house in Old Town Alexandria, and she had finally found a prospective buyer who was ready to make an offer. She invited me over for a celebratory dinner that evening.

"I'm just so excited!" my mother exclaimed. "After all my hard work, it's finally happened!"

"That's great, Mom! Where's the contract? Let's see it!" I said anxiously.

"Oh, he hasn't given it to me yet. He's going to fax it over next week after he meets with his accountant and lawyer," she said pouring herself another glass of champagne.

My mood immediately changed. "He hasn't signed yet?"

"Well, no, but he's already said he's going to take it. We've met several times; he's verbally told me he wants it, so the paperwork is just a technicality."

"Mom," I started carefully, "Let me tell you one thing I have learned in sales. Never assume anything. Until you have that contract signed and in your hand, you haven't closed the deal."

But my mom didn't want to listen. She was too busy dancing around the living room with her bottle of bubbly.

Two weeks later the deal still hadn't closed. But Mom wasn't stressing; she was absolutely certain that the paperwork was coming in any day. She decided to go on vacation to reward herself for all her hard work.

After almost a month had gone by, I stopped by my mom's house to see her. When I walked in, she was furiously cleaning her kitchen and hardly noticed me standing in the doorway.

"Mom? What's going on?" I asked. She only cleaned that vigorously when she was upset.

"I lost the deal," she said. "The buyer called me last night and said he got cold feet. I'm just so aggravated right now, I could scream. How could he tell me that he's going to take the property and then back out?" she said as she looked for something she hadn't bleached yet.

"Well, I hate to say I warned you, but until you have something in writing, you really can't count on it."

"I know, but he said all he had to do was go over some things with his lawyer and accountant and the deal was done."

"Yes, but so many things could have happened between then and now. You can't assume that everything will fall into place just because you want it to. I know you were getting all the right signals, but until the deal is signed, sealed, and delivered, you haven't closed it and you can't stop working at it."

Unfortunately, my mom learned the hard way that assuming the sale is dangerous. I have had many customers give me all the right signals, too. I've even had them tell me without a shadow of a doubt that they will buy from me. But I've also had those same people back out at the last minute. I have learned never to assume a deal is closed until the contract is signed and in your hand.

Assuming anything can be quite dangerous. There are many women out there spending their time with men they assume they will end up marrying. The signs are there: they are calling them, sleeping with them, maybe even living with them. But until a man has told you that you are The One, puts that ring on your finger, and says his "I dos," you shouldn't assume anything.

I finally thought Adison had found the right guy. Ben had his own software company, was smart, hardworking, and very affectionate. They hit it off right away, and Adison knew she was in love. She was dying to tell Ben how she felt but knew that she shouldn't be the first one to say it. So she held it in. Six months into the relationship they had their first big "relationship talk." Adison thought this would be it. He was going to tell her he loved her. She sat and listened as Ben struggled with the words. Finally he got to his point.

"I just think it's silly for us to have two places. You are here all the time. You go home once a week to pick up the mail and get more clothes. We are just wasting money paying two rents. I think it's better if you just move in here," Ben stated.

Adison was shocked. Not at all what she was expecting. Maybe a little more than what she was expecting. She just wanted an "I love you," and instead she got "Move in with me." Well, she thought, he must love me. He wouldn't have me move in otherwise.

She moved in. And for a while things were great. Six months later she still hadn't heard those three little words from Ben. But she did hear four other words: "Let's buy a house." Again, she thought he must love her or he wouldn't be doing these things. He was obviously scared to say "I love you" or maybe just bad at expressing his feelings. What's more important anyway? Saying how you feel or showing it? So they bought a house.

After living in their new home for a year, Ben told her one night that he really wanted to have a child. Now Adison was completely thrown off. She hadn't gotten an "I love you" or "Will you marry me?" but Ben wanted her to have his baby? She couldn't hold it in any longer. She had to say what she had been suppressing all this time.

"I love you," she declared. "I moved in with you, bought this house with you, all because I thought we were going to get married. But you have skipped over all the important parts of a relationship. You skipped the 'I love you' and now you are skipping the 'Will you marry me?' Why can't you say these things to me? It's obvious that you want them; I know I wouldn't be here if you didn't, so I want to hear you say it. You are going to have to start telling me how you feel instead of just having me read the signs. I want you to say you love me and want to marry me."

Ben didn't know what to say. At first he got angry. He tried to blame Adison for overreacting and being too emotional. But then he got very quiet and finally told Adison how he truly felt.

"Of course I want you here. I want you in my life and I think you would be a great mom. I just don't think marriage is for me, though. I am totally happy the way things are, and I see no reason to change them."

Adison felt like she had been punched in the stomach. She finally realized why Ben hadn't said he loved her. It wasn't because he didn't know how to say it. It was because he just didn't feel it. He loved having her around. He loved having her to hold at night. He loved having someone to eat dinner with and take on vacations. But he didn't want to fully commit to her. She had just assumed all along that he did.

I tried to tell Adison once that she shouldn't assume Ben loved her and was planning to give her all the things she wanted. She didn't want to listen, though. After she moved in and they started to house hunt, I told her not to assume it meant he was going to marry her. But she didn't want to listen to that either. Finally, after two years she realized what Ben really wanted. He wanted her to live with him and raise his kids without either of them having to commit to each other.

Assuming how a man feels is very dangerous. Sometimes you may be right in your assumptions, but if you are wrong, you may find yourself suffering the repercussions for a very long time. If Adison had told Ben that she was only going to move in with him if and when they were engaged, she would have avoided the mess she was now in. Maybe they would have gotten married, or maybe she would have had to move on, but either way she would be in a better situation.

Doesn't matter what stage of a relationship you are in—two weeks, two months, two years. You should never assume how a man feels about you. If he loves you, he will tell you. If you are his girlfriend, he will tell you. If he wants to marry you, he will tell you. If he doesn't say these things, it's a big red flag that you should worry about. Don't try to rationalize his behavior. Don't assume he isn't giving you what you want because he's had a bad past, a bad mother, or a bad ex-girlfriend. People do what they want to do. Likewise, they don't do what they don't want to do. It's just that simple. So when he says he can't do something or doesn't know how, it really means he just doesn't want to.

If you learn not to assume in your relationships, you will save yourself a lot of problems and heartache. People have different

motivations for getting involved in relationships, and some of
them don't have anything to do with love. A man can be lonely
and just want a companion. Some can even live with women
they have no intention of settling down with. Scary, I know. But
just look around—it happens to people every day. It has probably happened to your friends and even to people in your family. So you may have to ask yourself if it's happening to you.
It's not a pleasant fact to face, but you don't want to waste your
time with someone who ultimately won't give you what you
need. Remember: Just because he is dating you, sleeping with
you, or even living with you doesn't mean you should just kick
back, relax, and wait for the proposal. Until he's down on one
knee, ready to make it official, don't assume anything.

Fear of Loss

Jeffery and Camille have been dating for six years. They are
both thirty-five years old and live together in a beautiful town-
house outside D.C. For the last three years Camille has been
pressuring Jeffery to get married. She has brought it up several
times and has become increasingly frustrated with the situation. As we chatted one day, I asked her how long she would
wait for Jeffery before she came to her wit's end and moved on.

"I told Jeffery that if we weren't engaged by December then
I was leaving," she said. "I told him if he couldn't make a decision by then, I wasn't going to wait around any longer."

"Well, December is only two months away. I guess you'll have your answer soon," I said.

Camille laughed nervously. "Actually, that's what I said last year. The deadline was last December, not this one."

As I listened to Camille it became very clear. She would never leave Jeffery. She gave him a deadline but never followed through on it. She wasn't going to leave, and Jeffrey knew it. For the last several years he felt extremely secure about their relationship. He knew he wasn't going to lose Camille, so he knew he could keep putting off marriage. Camille got antsy and frustrated every so often, but Jeff knew that would eventually pass and she would still be there. Camille was in a terrible situation. Because she made it obvious that she would never leave, her only recourse was to nag Jeff to marry her. Unfortunately, nagging him wasn't going to get him to want to marry her. The most that it could ever do was annoy him so much that he'd finally break down and say, "Fine! I'll marry you." But who wants a proposal like that?

The number one rule in sales and negotiation is to be willing to walk away. If a customer knows that a salesperson will ultimately cave-in and give them whatever deal they ask for, they hold all the power and control in the relationship. There must be a fear that at some point the salesman will walk if he or she doesn't get what they need as well. This is called Fear of Loss (FOL). Fear of Loss is something frequently used in closing deals so that the customer doesn't end up taking advantage of the relationship. Jeff was not fearful of losing Camille, and because of it, he took advantage.

The Number One Motivator

I know we would like to think that all guys have the same marriage aspirations as we do, but some single men still need a little nudge down the aisle. Unfortunately, many women believe that showing a man all he has to gain from getting married will provide that needed push. But the fear of losing something is ultimately stronger than the sense of gain. Therefore, you will have to use this technique throughout your entire relationship with a man. You, too, have to be willing to walk away, and he has to know it.

If you are dating a guy who is more commitment shy than most, FOL is not only helpful; it's a miracle worker. Let me be very frank for a second. If a man knows he has your heart and soul, knows you would never stray, knows you would bear his children, and doesn't have to put your name on his checkbook, why would he? As unromantic as this may sound, taking a wife is like making a capital purchase. Unless you make more money than he does, he knows he will be sharing his hard-earned income with you. He will be the one bringing home the bacon, and you and the kids will be the ones to eat it. And if for some reason things don't work out, he runs the risk of you taking half of everything. This thought may have never crossed your mind, but believe me, this is something men worry about.

However, when a man meets a woman who knocks his socks off, a woman he's afraid he might lose if he doesn't treat her right, then he can't wait to get her down that aisle! He won't want to risk her leaving him for anyone else. He'll pay any price to have her and won't rest until he has closed the deal.

Think that sounds a little crazy? Most women are motivated to marry by FOL, too. Only it's not in the same way. I have girlfriends who are desperately trying to get married because they feel they are getting too old and they are afraid of losing their chance to land a husband and have children. They fear if they don't get married right now they will lose their youthful looks and their reproductive organs. So when they reach a certain age, some women just marry whoever crosses their path. Whether or not it's the right guy is irrelevant. They are so afraid of losing their opportunity to wed, they marry whomever.

Now that is what I think is crazy.

Fear of Loss vs. Sense of Gain

I myself have used FOL many times in business. When I was starting my own company, I had to hire a sales staff, and I had to do it fast. I packed in two dozen interviews one week in the hopes of finding great candidates for my team. To my disappointment, I found only one that really stood out above the rest. His name was Greg. He was a graduate of Harvard, young, ambitious, and above all, he had the attitude I was looking for. I wanted him on my team. I knew he would be a tremendous asset. The only problem was he had interviews with three other big companies the following week, and I was just a tiny business trying to stay afloat. I was fearful of losing him if he went on the other interviews and then I would have to hire my second choice. But what could I do? Try to convince him that we were the best company out there? Tell him how much I needed him? Beg him to forget the other interviews and shove a W-2 in his hand? He might have been flattered by it, but it wouldn't have made him want to work for me. No, none of that would work. The only thing I could do was use FOL.

I told Greg that I had to fill the position by Monday. I told him that I really liked him, but another equally qualified candidate was ready to start the very next day. I looked him straight in the eye and said, "Greg, if you can start Monday, you've got the job. If you still need time to think about it, I am going to have to go with the other candidate."

Now, of course, this was risky, but so was letting him go on his other interviews.

Greg shifted around uncomfortably in his chair. He let out a big sigh and shook his head. Just when I thought I might have made a mistake, he said, "Okay, I can start Monday."

Greg later told me that he really didn't have any other interviews. He only told me that to make him seem more desirable. How funny to think he was using FOL on me! I told him that it had worked.

It's a common philosophy for women to think if they promise a man the world, he will love them and marry them. I have seen friends and clients bend over backward for semiserious guys in an effort to get them to commit. It does not work. What does work is the attitude that you aren't sticking around if the situation is not going in the right direction. You have to have the will and ability to leave. Then, if and when things don't go well, you actually do it. I know it may scare you, but sometimes you have to leave in order to get someone to appreciate and respect you. I know your fear is that you will end up leaving and he won't come after you, but if he doesn't, then he wasn't going to marry you anyway, and you were essentially holding on to something that wouldn't have made you truly happy in the long run.

Creating Fear of Loss

So how do you create FOL? You don't want to threaten to leave your boyfriend every week, of course. And stating he needs to shape up or you will ship out is bad form too. If you are in a situation like Camille, you will eventually have to pack your stuff and make a move. But that's only if you have been dating and living with someone for years with no ring in sight. Otherwise you should be proactive with your FOL instead of reactive. Rather than wait until the end of the relationship, use it right from the very beginning. In the beginning you've automatically got FOL because the guy doesn't have you yet. Now all you have to do is keep it, which is much easier to do.

My friend Micha played it just right. She had dated a series of men, but none seemed to really float her boat. Then she met Brian. Brian was a little older, extremely successful, and looked like Hugh Jackman. She was a smitten kitten. I had never seen Micha, my business confidant and former boss, in such a giddy state. She once told me if things didn't work out with Brian, she would turn into a puddle, which is something so un-Micha-like to say.

Brian was smitten as well, and one night after only a month of dating he told Micha he was falling in love with her. He said he had never felt this way about anyone, which, of course, propelled Micha over the proverbial moon. She wanted to shout to the heavens that she felt the same way, but did she do it? Absolutely not! Micha is a saleswoman and a logical, strategic thinker. She knew Brian still needed to fear losing her. She told him she was flattered. She said she was enjoying spending time with him and felt very close to him. She did not tell him she was in love, too, even though she really was.

When I asked her why she held back, she said it was too soon to say it. She was ecstatic that Brian had professed his feelings, but she had to make sure they were deep-rooted feelings that would lead to marriage.

"I'm in for the long haul," she said to me one night on the phone. "He needs to be pining away for me. I want him to sweat. I want him to be crazy nuts for me and fear losing me to someone else. So, even though I want to start naming our unborn children, I am going to hold back."

Brian asked Micha to move in with him. But she declined his offer. She told him that she couldn't live with anyone she wasn't at least engaged to.

"It just wouldn't feel right," she said with a smile, then went away for the weekend with her girlfriends, leaving Brian to stew for the next three days.

When she returned, she found Brian on the beach waiting for her. He had set up a picnic on the beach to ask her to marry him. That was six years ago. Today, Micha and Brian live in a huge house in Santa Monica, and they just welcomed their third child.

Micha is no fool. She knew that she had to play a little FOL to really get Brian to make a move.

A man can tell you he loves you, tell you he is crazy for you, and then turn around a month later and leave you in the dust. If that hasn't happened to you, it's happened to someone you know. Just because a man professes his feelings fast and furiously doesn't mean he's going to end up popping the question. Sometimes it doesn't even guarantee he'll be around next week. Do not throw caution to the wind when you hear those three little words. Do not, I repeat, do not rest on your laurels just because a man says he's in love.

Throwing Away FOL

Let's look at how someone else handled a similar situation. Beth was in love with Rudy from almost the minute she shook hands with him. Rudy was tall, dark, and handsome, and basically swept her off her feet. After only a few weeks he told her he had never felt this way about anyone, and that he was falling in love with her. Overjoyed at hearing this, Beth told Rudy she was falling for him, too. They began spending all their free time together and were soon acting like a married couple, after only dating for three months. Beth started slowly moving into Rudy's house, leaving clothes and toiletries each time she was over. She would talk about where they would spend the holidays that year and where they would go on their next vacation. Then one day, almost out of the blue, Rudy told Beth he needed some space. He told her he wasn't sure if he was ready for "all this" and needed time to think. Beth was blindsided. She didn't understand what had happened. Just months ago he was professing his undying love, and today he was breaking up with her?

It was obvious Rudy began to feel stifled. He told Beth he loved her, but once he got her so quickly and completely, he lost interest. Because he never felt any FOL with Beth, he now was left just feeling trapped.

In the beginning, a guy may tell you he has very intense feelings for you. He's not lying. He probably does. He may use a number of different words to describe the feelings he's having; crazy for you, crazy about you, or maybe even in love with you. However, those feelings are not true love yet. How can they be? You have only known each other for a short time. Trust when I say the emotion a man feels at this moment is that of wanting, not love. Once you give in and give him what he wants, that craving will be over. That is what happened with Rudy and Beth. She assumed Rudy was really in love after just weeks of dating, so she let go and fell for him. Then, when Rudy came out of wanting mode and realized Beth was truly in love and he wasn't, he lost interest. I know it all sounds like a cruel case of bad timing, but if you can keep a little FOL while the guy is in his wanting phase, there is a good chance (if you are compatible) that the wanting will turn into love.

Rudy and Beth have been broken up for a while now, and Rudy is dating someone else. It may have worked out for the two of them if Beth had taken it slowly. When Rudy confessed his feelings, she should have told him she was flattered and having a good time with him. She should have kept FOL a little longer to let his feelings grow and develop. Instead, she let Rudy have her completely, and it destroyed the FOL, as well as their chance for marriage.

We All Make This Mistake . . . Just Learn from It

We are all giddy schoolgirls in the early stages of a relationship, and it's wonderful when the guy seems totally smitten with us. He says he loves us, and so we reciprocate. We immediately get comfortable and open up about our feelings. We fall in love, even though we've only known him for a few weeks. Everything is bliss for a little while, until suddenly he starts singing a different tune. He falls off the face of the earth, or worse, starts pulling back little by little (the slow fade is always worse, I think), leaving us to wonder what happened. Well, I will tell you what happened: we met him halfway. When he told us he was falling in love, we saw that as a green light to "let 'er rip!" We opened up completely and basically announced, "I'm all yours." That is where most of us make our biggest mistake.

You don't have to disclose your feelings just because he has. In the first couple of months especially, you have to keep that FOL for as long as possible. He can't know he's totally got you even though that is what he is asking for. It is easy to get caught up in a whirlwind romance, but you have to keep your head out of the clouds and make sound decisions if you want to take a relationship all the way to the altar. Don't assume the deal is done if a guy says he's falling for you. Know that you are on the right track, but continue to take things slowly so that you both develop a deep-rooted and lasting love. In dating, slow and steady always wins the race.

I'm happy to report that Camille and Jeffery are now engaged. After six years of begging and pleading she finally decided she was fed up and told Jeffery she was leaving. She said it was obvious he would never marry her, and she was ready to find someone who would. Jeff knew she meant it this time. Suddenly, he wasn't so complacent. Fearing he was really going to lose Camille, he hightailed it to the nearest Tiffany & Co. and purchased a two-carat princess-cut diamond. They are getting married later this year. Jeff never thought she would ever leave him, but once he was afraid of losing her, he moved to action. FOL gets them every time!

Sense of Urgency

A few months after my mother began dating my stepfather, Tim, she told him that she was thinking of moving to Florida. Her sister lives in West Palm Beach, and my grandparents are not far from there either. Tim didn't think much of it at first. They were just dating after all. But as Tim began to fall for my mom, she turned up the heat on the subject. One night she said to Tim, who at fifty-one had never been married, that she had found a condo in Wellington, Florida, and she was going to be moving at the end of the year.

Tim was shocked. "Are you really leaving at the end of the year?"

My mom just shrugged her shoulders and said, "Well, my kids are grown and away at school. The rest of my family is down south, and I really have nothing else keeping me here," she said as nonchalantly as possible.

She and Tim went to dinner that night. My mother chatted on about other things, but Tim kept thinking about what she had said. At the end of the night, he kissed my mom and drove home. The next time he saw her, he proposed.

No one knows how to date strategically better than my mom. She is a born salesperson and has taught me a lot of what I know. Tim, like many guys, was happy playing the field. He had dated many women in his lifetime and was very content not being married. Then he met my mother. Tim would tell you that unlike all the other women, she didn't pressure him for a relationship. She did the opposite! The real story, however, is that my mother knew how to pressure Tim without him actually feeling pressured. She used one of the oldest sales tactics there is. She created a Sense of Urgency (SOU).

What Is a SOU?

I know you have seen it on the Home Shopping Network— that little timer in the corner that says there are only five pieces of Jill Zarin's Skweez Couture left! You must buy them before the clock runs out or you will miss your chance! That little timer is creating a SOU. If the clock weren't ticking, no one would rush to order. You may see a product you like, but without a SOU, you could take your time and mull it over. There would be no pressure to make a decision, so you may never make one. Without a SOU, HSN would be out of business.

When you are dating someone, you absolutely need to create a SOU, especially if you want to take the relationship all the way. If you don't think your time is precious, then expect it to be treated that way. My mother knew how to create a SOU, and because of it, Tim proposed after only a year. But just like Fear of Loss, you can't only use a SOU when closing the deal; you must use it from "Hello."

SOU from the Start

I love being friends with Isabel because she is so easygoing and flexible. Anytime I call her, she's ready to do something. But that quality is often her downfall with men. When a guy calls, she is always open to doing something. If she has a previous engagement, she'll rearrange it to free up her schedule. The men she dates eventually become aware of this, so they don't feel any urgency to see her, call her, and finally, commit to her.

I've tried to explain to Isabel that if she's always "on call," a man will become less urgent about seeing her. Why would he be urgent? She will conform to his schedule. He can call at his leisure. Her time is irrelevant.

If you begin dating a guy and you constantly let him see you at a moment's notice, you are setting a standard that will become the norm. After you have been dating a while, he will become comfortable calling you at the last minute, changing plans on you, and even stalling on making a serious commitment. You have to create a SOU from the very beginning in order to set the precedent. Your time is valuable, and you have to be the first to treat it that way.

How to Create a SOU

When I ran my sales company, I was continually looking for new recruits every week. I had my receptionist screen applicants and book interviews. She was never to ask the candidate when they could come in for an interview because that would make our schedule look wide open. The perception would be that no one was interested in our position, and there would be no urgency to get the job. So I taught the receptionist to give candidates two choices. She would say, "Well, it looks like we only have two openings this week. Tuesday morning or Thursday afternoon. Which one works better for you?" The candidate would then have to fit into our schedule, which they always did. And not only did no one ever cancel, no one was ever late. People hung up thinking that we must be a great place to work, and the position must be highly competitive since those were the only two time slots open.

Create a SOU using the same strategy with men. For instance, when a man calls and asks you when you are free to see him, give him just two choices. Tell him, "I have a busy week, but I could do Tuesday or Friday night." Be smart about which nights you suggest. You want one of them to be a weeknight. Don't offer up both your Friday and Saturday evenings. When I started dating someone new, I kept my weekends to myself and gave the guy two weeknights to choose from. I wanted him to think getting a weekend date with me was tough, and I wanted him to suspect that I might have someone else in my funnel!

If you can fill up your week ahead of time so that you honestly do have limited availability for your dates, that would be best, but I know it's not always possible. Loading your week with plans can also be exhausting. It really does not matter whether you have actual plans or just your weekly date with Stefan Salvatore, just make sure that you still stick to a restricted date schedule for at least the first four weeks of dating. You should not be seeing each other more than once or twice a week in the first month. Seeing a guy too often (three and four times a week) goes against all laws of urgency. After all, how can a guy be urgent to see you if you were just with him yesterday? Space out your time together so that he builds up the desire to see you and continues to be urgent about it.

Your ultimate goal is to have the man asking when you are available. If he is the one telling you when he's free, you aren't creating enough urgency. When a guy calls you, the first question out of his mouth should be, "When can I see you?" If it isn't, you need to put yourself on a date diet and stop indulging him so much.

Using SOU to Close

There is a right way to close with urgency and a wrong way. It's vital to learn which is which, because you will ultimately need to use a little in order to get that ring on your finger. The wrong kind of urgency is asking repeatedly, "When are we going to get married?" or "I have to have kids by the time I'm thirty." It's also throwing out ultimatums and making demands. The kind of urgency you need to apply is indirect, covert, and circuitous. He must feel as if the pressure is not coming from your need to get married. No. Like my stepfather Tim will tell you, the urgency he felt was coming from the state of Florida, not from my mother. Never once did my mom tell Tim she wanted to get married. But he knew that proposing was the only way to keep her from moving at the end of the year.

When you close with urgency, the first and most important step you must take is to make a timetable in your head. Not the timetable of how old you want to be when you get married and have kids. For the love of Pete, throw that timetable out! This is different. You need to ask yourself how long you would date someone before deciding he is The One. How long do you need to be certain? Three months? Six months? After you have the answer, ask yourself how much longer you will date him before making your relationship official. A year? Two years? These are two very different questions, but you must have answers to both. Why? Because if you don't create urgency in yourself first, you won't ever be able to create urgency with him. Once you are involved in a relationship, it is very easy to let time slip away from you. You don't want to waste ten years with a man who is never going to marry you.

My mom's friend Dora has no SOU. She has been dating the same man for twelve years. Granted, he is a very lazy man with no real interest in having a family, so marriage is not a priority for him. She nags him every so often to get married, but he knows he really doesn't have to. He knows because she actually tells him. After every nag she says, "I don't want to push you; I want you to ask when you are ready." So basically her boyfriend has no real urgency to marry her. The clock's not ticking, so he's not popping the question. They will date until she actually does something to get him to propose. If she does nothing, he will never do it.

If you have decided you have found the right guy and you want to marry him, you need to decide how long you are willing to wait for him to propose. It doesn't matter what length of time you set (unless you want to get married next week. I'd advise dating a minimum of six months before becoming engaged). Once you decide on the timetable, you have to stick to it. If you think three years is long enough for him to decide and that deadline has passed, you have to have a serious conversation with him. Sticking around and giving him another year isn't going to do anything except make you angry. When a man keeps you past your expiration date, the relationship will start to sour. Every woman has a deadline in her head whether she acknowledges it or not. Most of my girlfriends end up staying way past their deadlines, and they end up in one of two places: either the relationship ends or they practically twist the guy's arm to get him down the aisle. By then he has made her wait so long that when the wedding finally comes, it's not a momentous occasion. It's just a relief he finally gave in.

You can easily avoid the above scenario. Once you decide on your timetable, do not share it with him. It won't do any good to tell him you will only date him for three years. The only thing that's important is for you to realize that a time will come for you to fish or cut bait. Once you accept that from yourself, as well as expect it from another person, your thoughts

will permeate your being. But it must be something you truly
believe and know you will honor. Then your expectations will
be heard loud and clear, without you having to say a word.
Most people don't realize how powerful their thoughts are. If
you think your boyfriend should propose and you know you
will ultimately find someone else if he doesn't, he will sense
that from you. On the other hand, if you have the "wait and
see" attitude, he will sense that, too, and I guarantee that you
will be doing a lot more waiting than seeing. Don't let yourself
be convinced that staying the course is ever a good idea at this
point. The longer you just wait and see, the longer you will just
wait.

The Silent No

After leaving my job to write this book, I thought I had said
good-bye to medical sales for good—until I got a call from
an aggressive recruiter named Christina. Christina was well
known in the medical community for having the inside scoop
on the hot sales jobs. She left me a message one day about a
"phenomenal opportunity" with one of the leading bed and
stretcher companies.

"Jess, it's Christina! Look here, I have a phenomenal opportunity with Stryker Medical. The reps are making a killing, the
territory is doing 100 percent over quota, and the rep in D.C.
was just promoted to management. This is a golden ticket! You

have to call me back as soon as possible!"

It did sound enticing, but I had mentally moved on from medical into other things. I decided not to call her back.

The next day I had another message on my machine from Christina.

"Jess, look girl, this opportunity is going to go fast! The rep last year became 'Rep of the Year.' What does that tell you? This is the dream medical job. Not a lot of prospecting, tons of repeat business, and a great company culture. Call me!"

After her second message I decided it couldn't hurt to call her back.

I found myself on an interview a week later. Christina called me Sunday night to go over some questions the manager would ask. On my way to the interview, Christina called again to make sure I was there on time and knew where I was going. I met with the territory manager for an hour and instantly established a great rapport. He asked me to come back for a second interview that Thursday, but, unfortunately, I was going to be out of town. He told me not to worry; he would have Christina call me when I got back in town to set up another meeting.

When I drove home that day, Christina called to see how the interview went. I told her it went so well that the manager asked me to come back for a second interview that Thursday. She was ecstatic. Apparently this manager never secures a second interview on the spot. I knew Christina really wanted to place me in the position because the payoff would be huge for her. We hung up the phone and she told me she'd call me after the weekend.

When I got back in town on Monday, I expected to have a phone call from Christina. The rules of recruiting etiquette are rather concrete. You always go through the recruiter. You don't talk directly to the company manager until after the third interview. But as I listened to my voice mail, I received no such call from Christina.

The following day I decided to send Christina an e-mail. I told her I was interested in the position and wanted to know if she had spoken to the manager about my second interview. I sent it off and waited for a response.

After no response by Wednesday, I realized what was happening. I was getting the Silent No. Christina had called me every day until I left town, and now she had literally fallen off the planet. The reason was simple: she didn't have any good news, and so she just didn't call me back. It's a classic sales move. Recruiters, and pretty much everyone else in the world, hate being the bearers of bad news. So when all you get is silence, you are really getting a "No."

It wasn't too much of a shock because when a customer decides that they are not going to buy from me, they avoid me like the plague. Christina practically stalked me to get me on the interview, and then after she had found out I wasn't getting the job, she disappeared. She had obviously talked to the manager, and even though he had originally asked me to meet with him again, something had changed in the meantime. He either met a stronger candidate or just decided that I was not a good fit for the position. Doesn't matter really what the reason was.

Either way, I wasn't getting the job.

There are times in dating that you too will receive the Silent No. When a guy suddenly decides he doesn't want to see you anymore, he may stop calling you as much, hoping you will get the hint. He may get busier and see you less but still pretend everything is just fine between you. This is because he doesn't want to have to spell out the obvious. What is a guy really going to say anyway? "Hey I was sitting here thinking about the last few weeks with you, and I realized that I really don't like you that much." Could you say that to someone? No, and neither can he.

The problem is that a lot of girls don't realize that a guy is trying to end the relationship with them. Some of us really believe him when he says he is just too busy to get together. We may then change our behavior to be more accommodating so that we can continue the relationship. If he stops calling us because he's super swamped at work, we start calling him. If he stops coming to our place because it's too far to drive, we hike over to his house. If he stops taking us out, we become content just sitting on his living room couch. In essence, we make it impossibly hard for a guy to break it off with us.

Willow had been dating Peter for almost six months. They lived in the same neighborhood and therefore could easily see each other. Things were going very well for a while, but then all of a sudden Peter's behavior began to change. He started to pull away. He wouldn't call or come by as much. When Willow called him, he wouldn't always pick up the phone. This went on for weeks. Willow didn't know it yet, but she was getting the Silent No. When she confronted Peter about his change in behavior, he told her he was just stressed at work. When she pressed the issue, wanting to talk more about it, he told her to stop questioning him and stormed off.

The relationship continued after that, and Willow thought Peter's moodiness would pass. She thought if he was stressed about his rigid schedule, she would do her best to be more accommodating. She offered to make Peter dinner at her house during the week so when he came home from work he didn't have to cook. But that didn't seem to alleviate anything. Peter would come by and eat, but wouldn't engage in much conversation. Usually he ended up going straight to bed. He would still sleep at Willow's place but stopped wanting to have sex with her. Of course, he attributed that to being tired from the day. At first Willow tried to sympathize, but the longer the relationship continued like this, the more upset she became. She called me frantically one night, looking for some advice.

"Willow, it sounds like you are getting the Silent No," I told her. "He doesn't know how to tell you he doesn't want to date anymore."

Willow had a hard time believing it, since Peter hadn't stopped seeing her completely. "Every Friday night he still comes over to watch a movie and fall asleep with me. Why would he do that if he didn't want to date me?" she asked.

"Boredom? Habit? Guilt? It's the easy thing to do? He'd rather hang out with you than go out to a bar?" I said.

Willow, of course, didn't like any of my answers.

Peter's actions continued to vacillate. One minute he was affectionate and attentive, the next he was moody and evasive. Sometimes he would come over and hang out, and sometimes he couldn't be found for days. Willow tried her best to be amenable for Peter, but after months of trying, the situation still didn't improve. The only thing that Willow knew for sure was that this wasn't the Peter she had been dating for the first six months. Eventually she told him she didn't think the relationship was going anywhere and that they may need a break. He told her that was probably a good idea.

You have to listen to a man's actions instead of his words, because a lot of time the no is silent. A girl can go on forever trying to please a guy who has already decided she isn't The One. It's a confusing predicament, I'll admit. We feel that if a guy doesn't like us, he will absolutely make a clean break. Why would he stick around and let us torture ourselves? Unfortunately, a guy can keep a girl around even if he doesn't have strong feelings for her. Why? Here are just a few reasons:

❶ **He's a coward.** It's easier just to keep seeing you than to tell you the relationship isn't going anywhere. He doesn't want to hurt your feelings, and God forbid if you cry or kill yourself over him. (Yes, some men have egos like that.)

❷ **He's bored.** He likes you but not enough to be exclusive with you. What if someone he really likes comes along?

He will hang out with you because you keep him busy on the lonely nights, while still allowing him to be open for other opportunities.

❸ He's insecure. You validate that he is a good-looking, worthy guy. He'd rather have somebody than be completely alone.

❹ He's using you. He calls when he needs something, and it's on his terms. He doesn't even have to convince you to do what he wants, you are happy to do it. He is a selfish person and you are not helping him break that habit.

❺ He's torn. He doesn't want to break up with you, but he doesn't like you enough to put more effort into the relationship. What if he lets you go but never finds anyone better? Below that tough exterior lies the heart of a chicken who is only worried about himself and his own future.

Don't fall victim to the Silent No. A man is never going to tell you, "Hey this has been great, but after dating for the last few months I realize that I don't really like you as much as I thought I did. You have a great body, which was what initially attracted me to you, but after getting to know you, I realize that I could never marry you. You are too high-strung, and I don't get your sense of humor. I wish you the best of luck, and I know that you will find the man you are looking for one day. I am just not him."

A man is never going to tell you that, and even if he did, would you really want to hear it? I honestly would rather not know the gory details. I'd rather hear the Silent No.

The Excuses

A lot of times the no is silent, but it is sometimes cushioned with an excuse. Some of the favorites are "I'm not sure I can handle my job and be in a relationship right now," or "My last girlfriend really scarred me, and it's making me fearful of getting close to anyone again." I've heard every antimarriage excuse from "I'm a commitment-phobe" to "I don't want to end up like my parents."

The problem is that when a guy says something like this, we think we can help solve his problem. If he is overworked and stressed, we think making a relationship easier will change his mind. We just have to be more understanding.

Likewise, if a guy says he's fearful due to a bad past relationship, we think convincing him that his ex was just a bad apple will help him realize we are not like her and thus make him feel comfortable enough to make a commitment again.

But counseling him on his issues and trying to change his mind won't do any good, because these are most likely not the real reasons he doesn't want to commit to you. Even if they were, how could you possibly help him get over something like his bad past? Are you a therapist? Even if you were, it would take years to help him work through his problems. Do you have years to spare? It's time to face the sad reality of the situation. Regardless of his excuse, the bottom line is that this man does not want to be with you anymore, and most likely he just doesn't want to tell you that his feelings have changed.

When my father finally decided to end his relationship with the woman who couldn't be herself, he was struggling with how to tell her it was over. He knew he wasn't in love and had already started chatting online with other women. After much contemplation, he decided to break up with her via e-mail. In the e-mail he stated that his previously failed marriages had made him commitment-phobic (which he knew wasn't the truth). He told the woman that he really cared about her and thought she was a wonderful person, but he was not prepared to commit to a monogamous relationship with her or anyone else.

With a severe case of anxiety, my father sent the e-mail. Not two minutes later, the phone rang. It was her. She had gotten the e-mail and wanted to talk. They met for lunch that very day. The woman showed up in tears, with the e-mail printout in her hand. My father agonized while she went through the e-mail line by line, debating each point he had made. At the end of the conversation she begged him to see a therapist with her. She truly believed if she could just get him some help for his commitment issues, she could save their relationship. My father, feeling trapped and horribly guilty for causing her pain, actually agreed to the therapy!

When I saw my father later that day, he was in shambles. He just wanted to make a clean break so he could date other women, but instead he was going to couples counseling! I had to laugh. I told my dad maybe he should be honest and tell the woman that he wasn't in love with her. My father shuddered at the thought and said, "I'd rather cut off my own arm than tell her that."

Don't make a guy spell it out for you. Be smart enough to know the specific reason he's giving you means absolutely nothing. The bottom line is he is breaking up with you. You are probably not going to get the true story from him, so don't waste your time trying to solve the lame excuse he came up with. If he truly loved you and wanted to be with you, he would be. End of story. It's not because you aren't a great person, because you are. And now that you are almost finished with this book, you'll be even greater! You just weren't a good match in the long run. Even though you didn't see it, he did, and you'll just have to accept it.

Buyer's Remorse

Maggie was in love with Sam from the moment she spotted him sitting at the bar in McCormick & Schmidt's. Not only was he the most handsome man she had ever seen in real life, he was popular and well liked by everyone. When Sam asked her to dinner, she felt like she had struck gold. How lucky she was that such a handsome and charismatic man was into her. She couldn't believe her good fortune.

Sam wined and dined Maggie for the first several months of

their courtship. Every weekend they would hit the town, going to the best parties and mingling with D.C.'s social elite. Most nights, they would end up having late-night drinks at McCormick & Schmidt's, the place where they first met and fell in love. Maggie was happy. She knew Sam was The One.

As the relationship progressed, Maggie started to settle down. She didn't want to go out as much and enjoyed staying home, renting movies, and cooking dinner. Sam, on the other hand, wasn't keen on the idea at all. He thought if he stayed home, he'd be missing something. It killed him not to be the life of the party, but it destroyed him to miss the party altogether.

After almost two years of dating, Maggie became distraught. In spite of all his partying, she still loved Sam and wanted to marry him. She just didn't know how to change his wild ways. Desperate, she sought me out for help.

"We've been dating for two years now and I know he is the one," Maggie said. "I just don't know how to get him to settle down and get married."

Knowing Maggie and Sam's relationship, I could clearly see a few problems that needed fixing. I also knew that as nice of a guy as Sam was, he was not really the one for Maggie. What was I to do? Fix her problem, or tell her she needed to find someone else? I decided I would do both, and let her decide.

"Maggie, you and Sam don't go two days without fighting. He's told you that you are too critical of his behavior. He knows you want to change him, but this is who he is, and he doesn't want to live his life any differently. If you really want to marry him, you have to accept that and stop telling him how much you disapprove of his lifestyle. For one month don't nag him about going out. Even if he doesn't come home until two in the morning, keep your mouth closed. If you do that, you'll stop fighting and things may improve."

"That's going to be tough," she admitted.

"I know, but if you don't do it he won't propose."

So for one month Maggie kept her opinionated mouth shut. She didn't nag Sam about hanging out at bars and going out with his friends. After the month passed, Maggie came back to see me. She burst into the restaurant grinning from ear to ear.

"It worked!" she exclaimed. "He said just the other day that we are getting along much better these days. He said he thinks we are finally on the same page!"

I tried to smile. "I guess as long as you can keep accepting him for who he is then you both will be fine."

I grabbed her arm before she could run off. "But I have to warn you of something, Maggie," I said in a very serious tone.

"What?" she asked sitting back in her seat.

"See that empty bar stool over there?" I said.

Maggie turned and looked.

"If you marry Sam, that is where you will be sitting for the rest of your life. If you are happy knowing you will always be chasing him in and out of bars, then go ahead and marry him."

Maggie thought for a second. Then she stood up, shook my hand, and thanked me for my help.

She and Sam were married six months later.

The wedding was the happiest day of Maggie's life. She had finally got what she had always wanted. Unfortunately, the minute they got back from the honeymoon, Sam immediately took off to McCormick & Schmidt's and was now staying out even later than before. Maggie had to call the bar so often looking for Sam that she had their number on speed dial.

Over the next seven years, Maggie and Sam struggled to get along. He continued to party and she continued to throw fits about it. She'd scream and cry; he'd yell and storm out. Every year was worse than the last. Maggie tried to bring up having a baby a few times, but since Sam wasn't home long enough to have a real conversation about it, she eventually dropped the subject.

On her thirty-ninth birthday, Maggie left Sam. She showed up at my house crying one night with her suitcase in her car.

"I left him," she said. "I just couldn't do it anymore."

I told her I was sorry. I knew this was going to be the most likely outcome, but I still felt bad.

"I should have listened to you," she cried. "You said I would be sitting on that bar stool, and you were right. Now I have wasted ten years of my life. I'm thirty-nine, and I don't think I'll ever have children."

Unfortunately, I had tried to warn Maggie that a marriage to Sam may not be ideal, but she didn't want to listen. She loved him and wasn't going to rest until she had him. So she took my advice, formed her strategy, and closed the deal. Now she was sobbing in my living room, suffering from the worst kind of buyer's remorse.

Buyer Beware

I can tell you how to find a guy. I can tell you how to meet him, get him interested, and finally close the deal. But the one thing that this book is not going to tell you is if he is the right one for you. That is something you will have to decide for yourself. These techniques are powerful. Remember that they are proven to work. So you have to make sure you are using them with the right person. Otherwise you could easily end up marrying the wrong guy and end up suffering from buyer's remorse yourself.

Jody wanted to get married so badly, it was all she ever talked about. She had every detail planned out, from the bridesmaids' dresses to the honeymoon destination. All she was missing was her groom. So, of course, when she started dating Vincent, he didn't stand a chance.

Vincent knew how desperately Jody wanted to get married. He would often tease her about it, and at one point even told her that he had bought a ring but hadn't decided if he was going to give it to her. After four years of dating, Jody was nearing the brink of insanity. One day while at lunch, she broke down and started crying out of sheer frustration.

"I have been waiting my whole life to get married! Vincent knows how important it is to me, and yet he keeps stringing me along, telling me he's not convinced we're ready. I feel totally powerless. What do you think I should do?"

"Jody, you need to play hardball with him. He has no incentive to marry you. You are basically married right now, just without the paperwork," I told her.

Jody nodded in agreement. "I can see that. So what should I do about it?" she asked.

"I think you should tell Vincent you need some space. Then for four weeks, don't talk to him or see him. Tell him that you have grown tired of waiting for him to make up his mind, so you are going to put some serious thought into whether you should continue this relationship or not. Don't answer the phone, and don't let him come over. If you do that for one month, and show him you take marriage very seriously, he will give you that ring," I advised.

As hard as it was, Jody followed my advice. She didn't see or talk to Vincent for thirty days. He tried calling her at home and at work numerous times, but she stayed strong. He tried dropping by in person, but she instructed her doorman to turn him away.

Then, exactly twenty-nine days later, Vincent sent Jody an e-mail asking her to join him for a very special dinner where he would ask her a very special question. She accepted the offer and was delighted when Vincent proposed that night.

When I saw her two months later, she was elated.

"Look at my ring! Isn't it gorgeous? I just can't believe it's finally happening! I can't wait to get married!" Jody said overjoyed.

"I am so happy for you," I told her. "So are you getting married in that chapel you told me about?" I asked.

"No, actually, Vincent doesn't want a big wedding, so we are going to go to Mexico and get married there instead," she said.

"Oh, well, that will be nice too. Are you still going to New Zealand for your honeymoon? I know how much you've always wanted to go there," I asked.

"No, Vincent thinks we should just stay a few days in Mexico to save ourselves the money. He really wants to put a swimming pool in the back of the house, so if we combine the honeymoon and the wedding, we can do that."

"Oh, I didn't think you wanted a swimming pool since you've always said they're a safety hazard for children."

Jody bit her lip. "Well, I do think that, but Vincent really doesn't want kids, so I guess it's not going to be a problem anymore," she sighed.

"Hmm . . . sounds like Vincent is getting everything he wants. No big wedding, no honeymoon in New Zealand, and now, no kids. I'm just wondering, Jody, are you getting anything you want?"

Jody looked at me and shrugged. She was so determined to get married that she was willing to give up all of her other dreams to do so. She left our lunch quietly, but I could see her mind was racing with a thousand thoughts.

Jody and Vincent got married in Mexico and installed their swimming pool. Almost immediately after the ceremony Jody began to regret her decision. Vincent was never flexible and only wanted to do what he wanted to do. Jody's wants and needs were often ignored or downplayed. Everything they did was for Vincent's benefit, never hers. Five years into the marriage, Jody finally decided to leave him. She had thought marriage was what she always wanted, but she was wrong. Being married to Vincent made her see that marriage itself is just a piece of paper. What she really wanted was a strong, loving relationship, which, from the very start, she never had with him.

Be very cautious, ladies. I know that many of you have dreamed of your wedding day, but just remember that day will come and go. The man you are marrying, however, will be there for the rest of your life. Marriage itself isn't a goal to be striving for. Marriage itself won't make you feel happy and complete. Jody made the mistake of thinking it would, so she married Vincent. She quickly learned just how wrong she was for thinking that.

People will give many reasons as to why marriages fail. I, for one, think the most common reason is because most people marry the wrong person in the first place. They have other motives for wanting to get married that ultimately cloud their judgment and convince them to accept a subpar or mismatched partner. Some people just don't want to be alone, or they simply want security. Others are tired of dating, or they feel societal pressure. These fear-driven motives cause people to reason their way into thinking someone is right for them when they are not. Even being in love with someone like how Maggie was with Sam can fool you into a bad marriage. Regardless of the reason, if you marry the wrong person, you have a long and arduous road ahead of you, and buyer's remorse is practically a given.

To me, no amount of money can compare to the value of happiness. When you get married you are basically paying the highest price possible because you are putting your happiness in the other person's hands. If you have the right partner, it's totally worth it. You are giving him all of you, and in return you are getting all of him. But when you have the wrong partner, it is certain disaster.

Women often think that marriage will complete their lives, and in essence, make them happy. But marriage (very simply put) is just a legal contract combining your assets and binding you financially to another person. There are no rules or guidelines that state how a husband and wife must treat each other. The relationship dynamic is made up entirely by the two people involved. Whatever the relationship was like before the marriage is assuredly what it will be like during it.

Think of marriage like a cake. You have to have all the right ingredients and measurements in order to have that cake bake properly. If you have too much milk or not enough baking powder, the cake won't rise or taste good. You will just end up with a cake pan full of mess in the end. The same goes for marriage. If you don't have the right ingredients to make the relationship work, the marriage will crumble into a mess as well.

Vincent and Jody did not have the right ingredients in their relationship, so their marriage didn't work. Jody was able to get Vincent to commit by using the techniques in this book. But these techniques won't turn a man into a kind and loving person if he isn't one to begin with. If the guy is wrong for you (or just a complete jerk), you have to be smart enough to see it. In both examples, the women wanted to marry men who were obviously not a good fit. One was a party boy, more concerned with drinking and socializing than having a relationship. The other was a selfish, greedy man who threw tantrums if he didn't get his way. They were both like this before they got married, and thus, they were still this way after.

Quality Customers

In sales we have what we call quality customers. They are the people who we know will absolutely benefit from buying our product. They are easy to deal with and make repeat orders, but most important, our product fits their needs. Unfortunately, there are some salespeople only concerned with making the sale itself. It doesn't matter to them if the customer is a good fit or not. They just want to make their commission, so even if someone is not a good fit, they will continue to sell them if they can. This is dangerous because there is a good chance the customer will experience buyer's remorse to some extent. They didn't buy the right product, but the salesperson was so convincing they purchased it anyway. After the deal is closed, they will call the salesperson with questions because they don't like or don't understand a particular feature. They get frustrated when they realize the product isn't exactly what they wanted. Finally, they end up complaining to everyone they know and eventually hate the product. Then, after all that is said and done, do you know what happens next? They make life miserable for the person who sold it to them in the first place.

Because you have learned how to close the deal on any man you want, you also must be careful that you don't close the wrong person. You have to be sure that you, too, are dealing with a quality customer—someone whose needs are met by your product and who meets your needs as well. Otherwise, you will suffer from buyer's remorse that will last for years and years. If you end up in a remorseful relationship, your partner is likely to be feeling the same regret. You probably know the old saying "Buyer, beware," but in this case, it's the seller who has to be careful.

On a positive note, I'm happy to announce that Jody met someone else a year after divorcing Vincent. She and Gary have been together for fifteen months are now planning the wedding and honeymoon that they *both* have always wanted.

CHAPTER EIGHT

maintaining the right mentality

Losing Him at Hello

One day I was sitting at a hotel bar in Chicago having a glass of wine when Isabel called. She was packing for our trip to Miami that weekend and getting excited about leaving town for a few days. But that wasn't all she was excited about. She was excited to see Doug, her new love interest who lived in South Beach. Doug and Isabel had been long-distance dating for a little over a month now, and she was starting to develop deep feelings for him. This weekend was supposed to be a girls-only trip, but it was clear that Isabel was going to break that rule. She wanted to spend as much time with Doug as she could.

"So what's your plan?" I asked. "Are you going to hang out with us or will you be glued to Doug the whole weekend?" I joked.

Isabel laughed. "You know me too well," she said. "I promise I will hang out with you girls. I just really miss him and want to see him as much as I can."

"I understand," I said. "So are you ditching us at baggage claim or will you at least make it out to dinner with us on Friday?"

Isabel hesitated for a moment. "Um, I'm not sure. I kind of want to get down there, feel things out, and then make a decision."

I was a little puzzled. If Isabel was so excited to see her boyfriend, why hadn't she made plans with him already?

"What do you mean?" I questioned. "You just said you wanted to spend as much time with him as possible. Now you want to get down there and see what's what?"

I should have known by the sound of her voice that something wasn't right.

"I do want to see him. I want to see him badly," she said. "But the thing is, the last time I was down there he said he thought we were moving a little fast. He said he had such a great time that it kind of scared him. So I'm not sure what to do at this point. I did talk to him yesterday, and he asked me what

I was going to do when I got here. I told him I wasn't quite sure yet, because what else could I say? I have to wait until he asks me to get together. I certainly can't pressure him about letting me stay at his place. Once he sees me, I'm sure he will ask me to, though. He's just being a typical guy right now."

As she was telling me the story, I knew what was happening. Doug wasn't being a typical guy; he was losing interest in my friend. He had come on strong in the beginning, but now his feelings were starting to fade. As an impartial bystander, I could clearly see what her next move should be. I wanted to say to her, "Isabel, just tell him that you are staying with your friends and that if he wants to see you, you'll be at the hotel."

But after knowing her for as long as I did, I knew she wouldn't do that. She liked Doug too much and there was no way she was going to take matters into her own hands like that, even though it was the smart thing to do.

"Here's my plan," Isabel proceeded. "I'm thinking we'll get there on Friday, and I will hang out by the pool in the afternoon with the girls. Doug knows when I am arriving, so he'll probably call then. I'll most likely meet up with him for dinner, and then I'm sure he'll want me to come back to his place."

The situation didn't sound good to me. If Doug really wanted to see Isabel, he would have already made plans with her. The fact that he was waiting until the last minute was a sign of low interest.

"Okay, Isabel, do whatever you want to do. Personally, I think you should make plans of your own this weekend because Doug has not made any with you. You should tell him what you'll be doing, instead of waiting around for him to make up his mind."

Isabel laughed nervously. "But the plan I want is to spend the whole weekend with him. Now that he's told me he's scared about his feelings, I can't push him. I can only wait until he's ready to see me."

"True, you can't make plans with him. You can make plans with us, though. Take some control back. I know you may not want to hear this, but if Doug says he's scared and isn't making plans to see you the few days you are in town, then he's probably losing interest in having a relationship. If he's backing away, then you should back away too. Tell him since he said he needs space that you've decided to hang out with the girls all weekend. If he really wants to see you, tell him you may be able to do dinner one night, but if he doesn't tell you soon, you are going to make your own plans. Use a little Fear of Loss. Then at least you won't have to sit around waiting. He will have one choice, and if he really likes you, he'll take it."

Isabel thought for a second. "But I don't want to only see him one night. I want to spend the whole weekend with him. If I say that I could be limiting my time with him. Also, I feel like asking him to decide right now is too demanding. He may still be freaked-out about things. No, I think it's best if I just wait for him to call and see what he says."

I gave up after that.

Regaining His Interest

It's always a little hard to accept that the guy you have been constantly canoodling with is beginning to lose interest in you. Most of us would rather turn a blind eye while praying to a higher power that the relationship will resume normalcy on its own. Some of us may take a more direct approach and launch a where-did-we-go-wrong interrogation, but the worst thing any of us can do is simply pretend that all is okay and convince ourselves that we are just expecting too much from a man. If a guy is beginning to pull away from you, the first thing to do is to admit that you have a problem.

When the guy you've been happily dating has suddenly changed into a cold and distant version of his former self, it is time to face reality. One of two things is happening: he is either reacting to something you did (such as gunning him down with all your bullets) or you are just now getting a taste of his real personality. Most women get extremely caught up in trying to figure out which one is occurring, but the fact is it does not matter why he is pulling away. Whether it's your fault or just his nature, you will still handle him in the same manner.

The first thing you want to do is follow the same instructions given in any crisis or emergency situation: Do not panic. If you begin to freak out and assume that you've lost your only chance at love, you will end up hurting yourself and possibly those around you (think of your friends and how much whining you'll put them through). Remain calm and don't make any sudden moves. Texting him for no good reason except to see if he'll answer and chat with you qualifies, so don't do it. When a man is losing interest, it is always safer to let him be the one to reach out to you. Start making plans with your friends, or begin that house project you've been putting off. Do something that can take your mind off your relationship, because the more you sit and think about it, the worse it will make you feel and the more likely it is that you'll do something you shouldn't.

Then from that point on, you want to start using the Mirror Theory for every move that he makes. If he doesn't text you for a week, you don't want to answer back for several days. If you meet up with him and he's clearly more standoffish than usual, you want to cease and desist all physical contact. Don't initiate a hug, don't rub his arm, and definitely don't try to get him drunk so you can make out with him one last time. If he tells you that he thinks you are moving too fast and needs a little break, tell him that sounds like a good idea given that the relationship is not turning out as you had expected. As much as it pains you, the only thing to do in a situation where you have lost a man's interest is to mirror his behavior. You don't want to overreact, but you shouldn't underreact either. Mirror Theory will help you determine just the appropriate response.

Isabel may have been able to turn her relationship around had she used Mirror Theory. She should have told Doug she was spending the entire weekend with her friends and pulled away from him just as he had done. She didn't have to be rude or snide about it. She could have politely said to him, "This is supposed to be a girls-only weekend, so I'll be making plans with my friends. If you want to have dinner one night, let me know, but otherwise I will be pretty busy." Even though it's not exactly what she wanted to do at the time, it was the only good move to make. Doing this would have allowed her to gain some ground back, put her in a less vulnerable position, and enabled her to see if Doug still liked her. If he took her up on her dinner offer, she would know more about how he really felt. She would have also gained more control over the situation and put herself back on equal playing ground. Remember, they had only been dating a month, so Doug should have still been in pursuit mode. When a guy stops chasing you it means he's losing interest, so the last thing you want to do is turn around and start chasing him!

The problem Isabel was having is that the move I suggested was in the complete opposite direction of what she wanted. She was hoping to spend the whole weekend with Doug. She thought that he would eventually make plans to spend a few days with her. To make her own plans meant she might risk not seeing him at all, which would then confirm her biggest fear: that Doug no longer wanted to be with her. So instead of doing what was smart, she kept biding her time and waiting things out. And you know what? When we arrived in Miami on Friday she stared at her phone all day and complained repeatedly about him not calling. Where was he? What was he doing? Why hadn't he called yet?

Eventually Doug did call her that night. It was around nine-thirty, and instead of mirroring his behavior, she ran to meet him. We didn't see her again until we boarded the plane on Monday. Seemingly, she got what she wanted—the entire weekend with Doug. However, the minute we got back to D.C., Doug sent her an e-mail telling her he just didn't think it was working out between them.

Keep Control, Keep Interest

Because Isabel had been doing nothing but waiting all day, she jumped when Doug called. If she had read his Buying Signs and accepted that his interest level had dropped, she could have better handled the situation. But instead, she ran to see him, which showed high interest on her part. That, coupled with the fact she spent all weekend with him, scared Doug off even further because her interest did not match his. And just so you know, when low interest meets high interest, a sunny forecast almost always turns gray and dreary.

I can't fault Isabel too much because I used to be just like her. If a guy began losing interest in me, I would sit around waiting to see what he would do rather than make a move myself. When I finally heard from him, I was so elated and relieved I forgot all about the fact that he was jerking me around. I would practically skip over to his house and jump into his arms, making no mention of how he ignored me for five days.

I held on to the hope that by some miracle his interest would reignite on its own and things would work out the way I wanted. I can tell you after dating this way for many, many years that never happens. The absolute worst thing you can do when a man loses interest is wait patiently for him to come around. Waiting for him to call after he's blown you off, or waiting for him to ask you out after he's told you he needs space, only ensures that you will do the wrong thing when the time comes.

Most girls only worry about gratifying themselves in the moment. They would rather do what feels good now instead of doing what will be best for the relationship later. Isabel got what she wanted in the short run—an entire weekend with Doug. But she ended up jeopardizing what she could have had in the long run—a serious relationship. Had she just tried taking control and mirroring Doug, she probably wouldn't have gotten dumped after the weekend. She may not have seen Doug while she was in town that time, but she would have probably seen him again. Now the relationship was completely over.

Nothing shows a man desperation more than having you jump to his attention after he's clearly flaked on you. He knows when he has let you down, so if you just accept it without a second thought, what impression does that give him? Doesn't it communicate a lack of self-worth on your part? Next time a guy says he will call and doesn't, remember that before you answer on the first ring.

Am I Crazy? Or Is He Moving On?

Sometimes it is hard to know if a guy is losing interest simply because you haven't known him that long. Typically you can tell a man is pulling away because his pattern will change, but what if you just met him a few weeks ago? What if he texted you for seven days straight and then skipped a day? Does that signify loss of interest? Most women will freak out at the smallest sign of a changed habit, but you cannot know a man's true pattern until you've dated him for a while. You need to observe him for at least a solid month before you can even begin to accurately sense a pattern. That is why it is so important not to panic or make any sudden moves at the first sign of disinterest. You could potentially react to a false alarm, which would then make you look crazy. In the beginning you just want to observe the guy and gather information about him. If he disappears for a day or two, don't assume you'll never hear from him again. He could very well be trying to hold your attention by being unpredictable.

If you have been dating for more than a month, and have collected enough data to write a thesis on him, there are a few telltale signs that typically indicate a guy may be moving on. Although it would be nice to get a Google alert when his interest tanks, chances are you are not going to be directly notified, so you will have to learn to read the signs of lost interest just like everyone else. Here are a few examples:

- He does not contact you for three times as long as usual. For example, if he usually contacts you every other day, he is now calling, texting, or e-mailing every three days.
- He makes plans with you and then forgets, or cancels them. For example, he says he wants to do dinner with you on Wednesday, but when that day comes, you don't hear from him.
- He starts making excuses as to why he can't see you. For example, work is getting busier (even though he's a third grade teacher and it's mid-August), or he has a sudden spike in social obligations and dates aren't welcome.
- He starts to nitpick everything. Whatever you do or say is wrong. For example, he is annoyed at how little you buttered the movie popcorn, or that you ran to the bathroom twice during the show.
- You are unhappy. You can't put your finger on why you think he's not that into you, but something deep inside has you uneasy. Trust your gut. If you feel more anxious than amorous, it is probably time to move on and find someone else.

It's always sad when the romantic bubble bursts and the guy you like stops liking you. Keep in mind, however, that hoping and praying he has a change of heart won't likely bring him back. But being smart and acknowledging the reality of the situation could. If you make the right moves and react appropriately to him, you will have a better chance at salvaging the relationship. The right move may feel as if it's pointed in the wrong direction, but I assure you, any alternate routes will only lead you to a dead end.

Don't Drink and Date

The best salesperson who ever worked for me was a twenty-five-year-old named Erin. Erin was a petite blonde with a personality that could fill a small auditorium. When she was hired, I knew she would be a high producer, but I had no idea that a third of my sales would come from this one little girl.

Every day Erin would return from the field with a stack of contracts. She outsold every other rep in the office by a mile. Some were extremely jealous of her ability. Others idolized her and wondered what her secret was. I, obviously, loved the girl. She boosted my sales and propelled me into a whole new tax bracket.

After Erin had been working for me for a few months, I started becoming friends with her, and one night she invited me out to a party being thrown by her boyfriend. When I arrived, I found Erin at the bar, smoking, laughing, and doing shots. I was a little surprised at first to see her downing hard liquor. I told myself it was her boyfriend's birthday and she was just celebrating. Really, *really* celebrating.

The next time I went out with Erin, she was celebrating again. But this time, it wasn't anyone's birthday. In fact, we were out with a bunch of coworkers at happy hour. She ordered several drinks and then eventually moved to shots. By the end of the night she was so drunk that she passed out in the bathroom upstairs.

I was conflicted. Here was this superstar salesperson who almost certainly had a drinking problem. I didn't know how serious it was, and I wasn't sure what to do. Then something happened that forced me to make a decision.

Since Erin was the rock star of the office, I often made an example of her. Two very important clients were coming to town and wanted to ride in the field with one of my reps. I saw no problem letting Erin handle that task—after all, they would be working during the day and nowhere near a bar. But as luck would have it, a huge snowstorm hit Boston that day and Erin was stuck three hours from the office with the two clients. I told her to find a hotel for the night. Their safety was first and foremost. I told her to take them out to dinner and be a pleasant, gracious, and sober host.

I worried a little that night, but there wasn't much I could do. The next day Erin made her way back to the office with the clients. When she walked through the door, I knew my worst fear had come true. Erin had a huge welt on her face that stretched from the top of her forehead down to her eye.

"What happened?" I asked in horror.

"Oh, I fell," she answered quickly.

"You fell?"

"Yeah, I fell. I dropped a piece of gum and when I went to reach down and pick it up, I fell."

Judging from the placement of the wound, I knew Erin was drunk when it happened. No one falls directly on their forehead when attempting to pick up gum.

"So you tried to pick up gum and did a face dive into the pavement?"

Erin smiled sheepishly. "You make it seem so much worse than it is. I'm just a klutz. I fell," she said picking up her bag and inching toward my door.

"Don't you go anywhere. Go hang out in the back office until I come get you," I told her.

I asked the two clients to sit down with me. They confirmed what I had suspected. They had gone out to dinner, and Erin started drinking. She drank so much that she was slurring her words, dancing on her chair, and even tried to kiss one of them. I was mortified.

I had very high hopes for Erin. She was a phenomenal salesperson, and I had hoped to promote her into management at the end of the year. My goal was to open another office and have her pioneer it. Now, not only was I not promoting her, I was going to have to fire her and somehow get her to seek help.

When Erin was terminated, it shocked the rest of the office. Most of them never even knew why I let her go. Those that did couldn't believe how she could jeopardize her job like that. How could she take out two clients and behave so badly? Didn't she realize she was representing the whole office? Didn't she realize how important it was to make a good impression?

As crazy as it sounds, everyone I know has at some point made the same mistake as Erin. They may not have endangered their jobs by drinking with clients, but I know many women have jeopardized their relationships by drinking on dates.

Drinking While Prospecting

Melinda is a hopeless case. She wants more than anything to find a husband, yet she continuously sabotages her own chances at getting one. Every time she goes out prospecting, Melinda drinks too much. She tells me going out to a bar is unbearable without a cocktail or two. Usually she meets a guy early in the night, while she's still semisober. They talk, joke, and generally seem to get along. If Melinda were smart, she would give the guy her number, end at the Height of Impulse, and take herself home. But she's not smart. So instead she keeps drinking, goes home with the guy, has sex, and never hears from him again.

I continually tell Melinda she needs to stop getting drunk. Does she listen? No. It's not because she can't stand going to bars without drinking; it's because she's insecure and afraid of rejection. As far as she's concerned, the alcohol transforms her. When she's drunk she becomes the hottest woman on Earth. Unfortunately, she becomes the sluttiest woman on Earth as well.

When you are prospecting, you must be careful not to sabotage your own chances at finding someone. If you are out at a bar or club, it's easy to lose count of how many drinks you've had. Melinda never plans on getting drunk. However, when she gets there it's a different story. She gets caught up in the moment. She meets a guy, likes how she is feeling, and doesn't want to lose it. He keeps offering to buy another round, and she can't refuse. Before she knows what's happening, she's making out with the guy in the middle of the club as her friends watch, shaking their heads.

This has become a very destructive pattern for Melinda. It's a shame because she is a phenomenal prospector; she just lacks the discipline needed to close the deal. For years I've watched her do what feels good and have seen her make the same mistake over and over. Unfortunately, she's not the only woman who does this sort of thing. There are lots of women out there who don't realize how drinking skews their judgment. They wake up the next day wondering why the fabulous guy they had so much fun with last night didn't want to see them again.

Drinking on a First Date

The only thing that's worse than getting drunk while prospecting is getting drunk on a first date. My friend Katherine is stunningly beautiful. Not only that, she's sweet, funny, and has a lucrative job selling private airplanes. She's very busy during the week and even on the weekends, so she uses eHarmony to prospect for men. She usually sets up her dates in the evening instead of doing coffee or lunch. I thought this was fine, until I realized why she was doing this. Katherine needs to drink on her dates. She is nervous about meeting men she doesn't know and needs something to take the edge off, which is not a horrible thing by any means. I agree that it is nerve-wracking to meet someone new for the very first time, and having a glass of wine is usually pretty harmless, as long as you are twenty-one and not driving.

But one day when I was at lunch with Katherine, I realized something. She had met ten guys on Match.com within the last couple of months, and not one meeting resulted in a second date. I thought it was very strange given the fact that Katherine is such a catch, as well as a professional salesperson. She should know the dos and don'ts of getting a man interested. So why hadn't any of her first dates come back for seconds? I had her tell me exactly what happened on each of her dates to see if I could figure out what the problem was.

As she relived each encounter for me, nothing she said seemed out of the ordinary. She said she would meet for drinks, usually get some dinner, maybe grab another drink afterward, and then go home. She didn't talk about her dreams of four kids and a minivan, and she didn't unload any personal problems. Everything she told me seemed completely fine.

Then a few weeks later, I was at Barnes & Noble, and I ran into a guy I used to know in college. We got to talking, and he told me he had been trying online dating. I asked how it was going, and he told me for the most part it was great. The only bad date he had was with a superattractive girl who sold airplanes. Of course, I almost choked on my latte when he told me that. There aren't many people in that industry, so I had to ask what her name was. He said it was Katherine.

He told me that the date started off great. They met at a martini bar in the city and had a couple of drinks. He was really attracted to her at first. They went to dinner at a little French bistro and Katherine ordered another drink. It was shortly after that when the date started to go sour.

"Jess, it's such a shame," he started. "After a couple of drinks she starts swearing like a sailor. It's the most unattractive thing. She is such a beautiful girl, but after a couple of drinks she started dropping F-bombs. And it wasn't just one or two; it was every other word! I think she even swore at the waiter."

"Oh my goodness," I said. "That's terrible. You must have felt so embarrassed."

"I did, but the worst part was I thought I could actually like her. When I saw her I was immediately attracted to her. Then she opened her mouth and showed me that she had no class. I can't date a girl with a mouth like that. It's such a turnoff."

I thanked my friend for telling me the story and rushed home to call Katherine.

She didn't realize she was doing it and she wasn't a classless person, but whenever she had too much to drink, Katherine became a potty mouth.

Sometimes drinking not only causes you to lose your inhibitions, it can also make you do or say certain things that just aren't appropriate on a first date. Katherine knows how to close the deal with guys. She understands the strategy and how to execute it. But with each drink she has, the strategy becomes less important and harder to stick to. She says what's on her mind, and she says it with . . . um . . . conviction? She's enjoying herself and does not realize how her behavior is affecting her date.

I know when you go on a date you may be a little nervous. I know that having a drink or two can take the edge off, and like I said before, I see nothing wrong with it. The problem is that some women don't know their limits. They think the date is going well because they are having a good time, and if they are having a good time, then the guy must be, too. But alcohol can give you a false sense of confidence, and it makes it impossible to think logically or to see the reality of a situation. When you drink, all awareness evaporates and you are basically dating blindly.

The Drunk Dial

Perhaps the most dangerous and most common of all dating pitfalls is the dreaded drunk dial or text. No good can ever come from either. It can cause sudden, instant, and otherwise immediate death of a relationship.

Case in point: Jenny met Jeremy at a bar one night. They were both there for a happy hour thrown by a mutual friend. They struck up a conversation and ended up flirting with each other throughout the night. Jeremy told Jenny she was cute and fun to hang out with but didn't ask for her number.

The following week Jenny ran into Jeremy again. This time, at a going-away party. They hung out together for most of the night, and when the party wound down, they decided to continue the good time at a local pub.

At the end of the night, Jeremy still hadn't asked for Jenny's number. But he did tell her about a barbecue that weekend being thrown by one of their mutual friends. She told him she would come and bring some girlfriends with her.

At the barbecue, Jenny and Jeremy got very flirty and even made out in her car at the end of the night. He finally asked for Jenny's number and told her he would like to go out to dinner with her sometime during the week. Jenny suggested Wednesday, and Jeremy agreed.

Wednesday rolled around, and Jeremy texted Jenny. The text said he had gotten invited by an old friend to a Nationals game and couldn't make dinner. He apologized and said he would call later in the week to reschedule. Jenny was disappointed. She felt blown off, especially after kissing him at the barbecue. She decided to go out with her girlfriends that night and ease the pain with some sake bombs.

Jenny told all her friends about Jeremy. She told them they had kissed that weekend, and then he blew her off for dinner in a text message. They were all angry and told Jenny he was a jerk. They told her not to let him treat her like that and to ask him what the hell was going on with the two of them. Why did he wait so long for her number? Why did he kiss her and diss her? What were they doing anyway? Dating? Just messing around? They told her she needed to find out.

At two-thirty in the morning, Jenny reached for her phone. Totally wasted from the night of sake bombs, she dialed Jeremy's number. He answered. The conversation went something like this:

"Hey, it's Jenny. What are you doing?"

"Huh? I'm sleeping. It's two-thirty, and I have work tomorrow."

"Oh, well, how was the game? Was it worth ditching me for dinner?"

"Uh, it was good. I'm sorry about that. I did want to go to dinner, but my friend was only in town that one night. I was planning to make it up to you this weekend."

"Well, I think that was a total asshole thing to do if you ask me. What are we doing anyway? What are we? Are we dating or are we just going to be friends that mess around? Cause I am not like that. I need to be treated with respect."

"Uh, okay."

"'Okay?' That's all you have to say for yourself? What are you trying to do here, Jeremy? What exactly is it that you want from me?"

"Well, right now I want you to let me go back to sleep."

"Oh fine. Go to sleep, just know that you are on thin ice, buddy."

And with that Jenny hung up.

The next day Jenny hardly remembered the conversation. She got to work and logged on to her computer. Not feeling that well already, she checked her e-mail and saw Jeremy had sent her a message. He said he was sorry for making her upset. He also told her he was not looking for a relationship, and that he really didn't appreciate the 2:00 AM phone call. He told her he thought she was a nice girl and he wished her the best of luck in the future.

The Sobering Truth

Jenny totally blew it. If she had read the signs, she would have seen that Jeremy had moderate interest in her. It was too early in the relationship (they hadn't even been on one date yet) so she really had no right to call and chew him out like that. She should have acted more indifferently, held back the makeout bullet, and used more of a SOU. She should not have gotten drunk, called him up, and asked point-blank what his intentions were. That took Jeremy's interest from moderate to nonexistent.

The drunk dial is dangerous because in one fell swoop, you can ruin your chances with someone. Alcohol and cell phones are a toxic combination. For some reason when women get drunk they love to pick up the phone and contact the one they love. Unfortunately, they don't realize that getting too drunk always leads to vomiting . . . the verbal kind at least.

In order to really be able to follow the techniques in this

book, you will have to take alcohol out of the equation. If you are the kind of person who can't just have one drink, then no matter what you have learned from reading this, you will not be able to land your man. Just like emotion clouds logic, so do martinis. There is no way you will be able to think logically and strategically if you are intoxicated.

Don't feel bad. Lots of women have this problem. I have girlfriends and clients who know how to close the deal but still drink too much and ruin their chances. They wake up the following day fully aware of what they did wrong, and yet they will go out the next night and do it all over again. You are definitely not alone if this sounds like you. Now you just have to recognize that it is a problem and discipline yourself to change it. Drinking and dating is very common and very dangerous. If you know you cannot limit your alcohol intake, the best advice I can give you is to make your dates during the day. Do coffee or lunch. Maybe try an activity like rock climbing or hiking. If you are doing some activity other than just standing or sitting around, you will likely not feel the urge to drink. Besides, there aren't many places to get beer on the way up a mountain.

Be smart: don't drink and date. You could ruin your chances of hitting it off with a great guy if you do. You need to keep your head straight and your mind clear. If you know of a girlfriend who also has this problem, it is your responsibility to warn her as well. Friends don't let friends drink and date either.

The Waiting Game

When I was younger, I dated a guy who worked on a local morning radio show in Washington, D.C. We dated for a couple years and broke up over something so trivial I can't even recall what it was now. After spending a month apart, I ran into him at a fund-raiser for missing children. Instantly I knew that I wanted him back. He looked great. He had been working out, he had let his hair grow longer, and he was sporting a five o'clock shadow. But it was more than just the appearance that reeled me back in. After talking to him for twenty minutes, I remembered what a great guy he was, and how silly our breakup had been. I hesitantly left the event, hoping that he would call me.

I got home that evening and physically wrestled with my phone. I wanted to talk to my ex, but I knew that the ball was in his court. He would have to call me. I had to resist. I called everyone in my phone book to avoid dialing his number. I talked to my mom until I fell asleep on the couch. As hard as it was, I went to bed that night without giving in to my impulses.

Monday morning I got up and went to work. I logged on to my computer to check my e-mail, and lo and behold, there was an e-mail from my ex. Thank God I hadn't given in! The waiting game paid off. As difficult as it was, I made the right move and a week later my ex and I got back together.

I know I said that prospecting was the worst part of being a salesperson. Well, I lied. The worst part is the waiting game—

the period of time when you can do absolutely nothing but wait for the other person to make a move. That is the worst part by far.

Luckily, I only had to wait a weekend to hear from my ex. But sometimes the waiting game goes on for weeks and even months. It's a tough thing to do because the situation is completely out of your control. It's not fun, but here's why it's necessary that you don't give in.

The worst salesperson I ever met worked in my office in Texas. He was notorious for screwing up his own deals. He would find a customer who was interested, but ultimately he would always foul it up somehow.

One of his customers was a busy doctor. The salesperson wanted to switch his phone carrier, but the doctor wanted to wait and see his next phone bill first. The salesperson knew the doctor was interested and didn't want to let the sale slip away, so he created a SOU and told the doctor he could give him an even better long-distance rate if he signed up by the end of the day. The doctor toiled a few minutes thinking about it. Just before he could answer, a nurse popped her head in and needed the doctor for a minute. He excused himself and told the salesperson he would be right back.

Alone with his thoughts, the salesperson started to worry that he had pressured the doctor too much. What if he came back and said that he'd passed on the deal altogether because he couldn't make a decision that soon? He did say he needed to see his next phone bill. What if he needed until the end of the month to get that bill? When the doctor returned, the now freaked-out salesperson jumped up and said he could give him until the end of the month to make a decision. When the doctor heard that, he was surprised and caught off guard. He told the rep he was going to buy today, but if he had more time to decide, he would think about it further and wait until then.

Had the salesperson just played the waiting game and stuck to his first offer, he would have closed the deal that very day. He had created urgency in the doctor, but then got nervous and recanted. He didn't have the discipline or the confidence needed to wait and see what the doctor was going to say, and he lost the deal because of it.

Women sometimes get the same itch. They drive themselves bananas while sitting around waiting for a phone call. They climb walls waiting for their latest strategy to play out. They want answers and they want them ten minutes ago. Understand that sometimes you will be in a situation where you really can't and shouldn't do anything but wait. Think of it like a game of chess. You make a move, and then you have to wait until the other player makes his. You cannot get impatient. He may make his move right away, or it may take him a while. Either way, you cannot make another move until he does.

Don't Sweat the Techniques

Paige was dating a guy she really liked. Tyler was a tall, charismatic guy with sparkling blue eyes. Everyone he came in contact with liked him instantly. Paige had a lot of competition. The two had been dating for several weeks, and Paige was really starting to fall for him. The problem was that Tyler wasn't exactly acting like he was in love. He would call her, but it was sporadic. He would take her out once a week, but on other days, she never knew where he was. She felt totally powerless and out of control. Since she and Tyler's dates were so few and far between, she always jumped at the chance to see or talk to him. After almost two months and no change in interest level, I told Paige that she needed to change her course of action. The relationship was not progressing, so it was time to take action in order to move it one way or the other. The next time Tyler called and asked her out, she needed to tell him she was busy. She needed to create a little SOU and have him feel a little FOL. Paige was terrified to do this. What if he felt rejected and never called again? I convinced her that this was the best course of action and that what she'd been doing all along by being so available was even riskier than what I was suggesting.

When Tyler called that Friday, I sat there and coached Paige on what to say. She declined his offer to take her out on Saturday. She nicely told him she had other plans and maybe they could go out some other time. With that, she hung up.

A couple of days went by, and Paige was an emotional wreck. She walked around like a zombie. She continually asked me if I was sure the strategy would work. I told her that it would, but in the off chance that it didn't, it meant Tyler didn't really

like her anyway. She continued for the next few days to wrestle with her feelings. Then just as she was about to reach the brink of insanity, Tyler called. He told Paige how much he missed her and needed to see her. This, according to Paige, was something he had never said before. She was elated. The waiting game had paid off.

Like most girls, Paige was terrified to make her own strategic moves. She was worried about the consequences of her actions. In essence, she was happier not knowing how Tyler really felt about her because she would rather have a small piece of him than none of him at all. She worried that making this move would tell her what she feared—that he didn't really like her. She would actually rather lie to herself and keep seeing him than get the truth and have to stop.

Sometimes it may be scary to use the tactics you have learned in this book. If a guy truly doesn't care about you and is at the point of using you at his leisure, then the tactics honestly may not work. But do you really want to be with someone who considers you an occasional pastime? These techniques are designed to get you what you want, but they are also designed to get you answers about a man's real feelings. Just remember, after every strategic move, you are going to have to play a little waiting game. Don't freak out. Be confident in your logical decision making. Trust in the techniques that have been proven to work for centuries. Don't make a move and then make the mistake of counteracting it. Sometimes all you can do is wait. It may be agonizing, but it's necessary.

When Waiting Pays Off

Helena, a client of mine for many years, showed up one day at my office in shambles. She had gone on two dates with a man named Jim who she really liked. The problem was that Jim was in the middle of a messy divorce. Although he wanted to date again, he was still having trouble getting over his failed marriage. After their second date, which according to Helena went extremely well, he promised to call and make plans for the weekend. When Saturday rolled around, however, Helena's phone didn't ring. She decided to send Jim an e-mail just to touch base. He wrote back apologizing for not calling her when he promised, but made no mention of seeing her again. Helena was very confused. She asked me what she should do from here because he didn't ask her any questions in the e-mail, and it was clear they weren't going on a date that weekend. I told her to do nothing. She could write back that she accepted his apology but beyond that she would just have to wait to see what he would do from here.

As sad as she was and as much as she wanted to try to control the situation, Helena did nothing. As another week passed, she found herself itching to contact Jim. Maybe he just needed a little encouragement? Perhaps he's just been out of the dating game too long? In the end, Helena resisted because she knew that whatever was going on with Jim had nothing to do with her. They had a good time on their date but he probably just wasn't ready to get involved with someone.

Three months later, as Helena was sitting at home one night, she received an unexpected e-mail. It was from Jim! He apologized profusely for his past behavior and told her at the time he just couldn't begin a relationship with one person while he was still ending one with another. He told her he would love to take her out again if she would let him. They are now happily dating.

Had Helena not played the waiting game, she may have pushed Jim into seeing her when he was not ready. She may have chased him away because he was not at a point where he felt comfortable pursuing a relationship with her. Thankfully, she just waited for him to make the next move when he was ready, and it paid off.

It's important to remember that just because a relationship doesn't happen right away doesn't mean it won't ever happen at all. Helena had to wait three months for Jim to come around, but sometimes you may have to wait even longer. Remember that men have things going on in their lives that may ultimately put dating you on the back burner. Timing is a very important and uncontrollable factor. If you try to control it, you may end up ruining your chances to rekindle the romance later.

No Means Next

I remember when I first started in sales I would spend days in a customer's office trying to convince him or her to buy from me. Often I would go back to see the same person who had callously turned me down the week earlier, in an effort to change their mind. I spent an exorbitant amount of time with people who just weren't going to buy from me. Then I realized that my time was much better spent moving on to find someone who would.

In sales, we believe you should take three "no's" and then leave. If you hear no once, then it could be you haven't done a good job getting the customer's attention and you need to change your approach. If you hear no for the second time, you may need to provide more information or figure out another angle to take. But if you hear no for the third time, then believe it to be a true no. After the third no, you are wasting your time with someone.

Sometimes it doesn't matter how good of a salesperson you are. Some customers just aren't meant to be sold. It has nothing to do with the product, the presentation, or anything else in your control. You won't be able to sell 100 percent of the people 100 percent of the time. So the best thing to do is move on when you get to that point. Don't make the mistake of thinking everything is within your control. Some things are not and you have to accept that.

When my friend Cobie started dating my other friend, Rob, I was really excited, as were the rest of my friends. We all thought they were great people whose relationship could potentially go the distance. But Rob and Cobie had some very big lifestyle differences that would have to be resolved if they wanted to take their relationship all the way. Rob was extremely type A and a self-proclaimed neat freak. Cobie, on the other hand, was often referred to as "Hurricobie," due to her messy tendencies. Rob was a real early bird, whereas Cobie was often advised not to drive or operate heavy machinery before noon. I remember saying to one of my friends about their relationship, "This will either end badly or not end at all." Ironically, I was right on both accounts.

Rob and Cobie's relationship was great for the first few months, but once the summer ended, things began to get stormy, and it seemed like Hurricobie was about to strike again. Rob could not put up with Cobie's lax attitude toward tidiness. He thought it was disrespectful when she failed to pick up after herself when she stayed over. He also felt that waiting until noon for her to wake up was ridiculous. He liked to get an early start on the day and became grouchy when he could not do that. He called Cobie a "teenager" and told her he felt less like her boyfriend and more like her dad. He broke up with Cobie, citing that they were just too different to make things work.

Cobie tried desperately to get Rob back, and it worked. She would beg and plead and tell him she would change, but in the end, she always fell back into her old patterns. Rob continually broke up with her, and Cobie continued to hang on to their relationship for dear life. She just could not accept that Rob wanted to end the relationship, even though he had said no to it several times. In the end, they wasted almost five years of their lives because Cobie refused to take no for an answer and move on.

Dealing with Rejection

The word "no" can be hard to handle. When I first heard no from people, it really affected me. I took it very personally. I wondered what was wrong with me. *Why didn't this person like me?* But then I realized that no was not personal. It didn't mean I had failed, and it didn't mean I did anything wrong. No did not mean that I was being rejected.

It's normal to feel that way when a relationship doesn't work out. Even if you are the one who ultimately ends it, you can still feel rejected. But you have to have the mentality that it is not personal. I know right now you are thinking, *How in the world can it not be personal?* Well, you have to stop thinking that a man not wanting you is a reflection of how good of a person you are. It's not. If your relationship doesn't work out, and you have played by all the rules, it's because it wasn't meant to work out. You were meant for someone else. He was meant for someone else. You are both good people who just aren't good together.

Although you may love someone and not understand why you're not right for them, you have to trust that they know themselves well enough to figure out what kind of partner they need. If they don't think that you are the right type for them, you have no choice but to just accept it. That's the mentality you must have.

Anne once dated a guy who started out as a friend. He had liked her for years and finally convinced her to give him a shot. They dated for six months, and he was totally and completely in love. But after the crazy infatuation subsided, he started to really look at Anne as a life partner, and wondered if she was the right fit for him. They had very different belief systems and very different goals for the future. So even though this guy was crazy about Anne, he broke up with her. Of course, Anne felt completely rejected. How could this guy love her for five years, finally get her, and then dump her? What she didn't understand was that he wasn't rejecting Anne as a person. He truly had feelings for her. He just didn't think that in the long run they were right for each other. He needed someone who wanted to stay home, cook dinner, and raise kids. The only thing Anne ever wanted to make for dinner was reservations. Stay home and raise children? That's what nannies are for! So even though he really liked Anne as a person, he had to let her go. It was as rough on him as it was on her, but it was ulti-mately the right decision. They both ended up marrying other people years later.

When a relationship ends, most women feel they did some-thing wrong or just weren't good enough to keep a guy's inter-est. That isn't always the case, however. You have to realize that not being good as a couple doesn't mean you aren't good on your own. You cannot be everyone's type, and it is egocen-tric to believe you are meant for every guy you set your sights on. Loving someone is only a small portion of what makes a relationship run smoothly. You have to have common morals and values, complimentary personalities, and a variety of other components. If someone breaks up with you, it has nothing to do with your worth as a person. You simply don't match in one of these areas.

As long as you go back to prospecting, you will find another interested guy. It's inevitable. So don't fret about moving on because you fear you will never meet someone else. You just need to go back to the basics. Prospect, fill your funnel, and keep a positive attitude. You are in control here. So if you want to meet someone else, you will.

Practicing in Gamelike Conditions

Adison had just finished reading the rough draft of this book and couldn't contain her excitement. She finally realized what she had been doing wrong, and now had an action plan on how to do it right. After taking a yearlong hiatus from dating, she was ready to get back out there and put what she had learned to good use. She told all her coworkers about the techniques, and they decided to practice among themselves during their lunch break. They took turns walking by and giving each other the SEE Factor. They practiced their Icebreakers, and they would mirror each other's body language. They were all confident and assertive. They felt good. Enough of the dress rehearsal—they were ready for opening night!

They decided to go to a very well-known bar downtown. After ordering their drinks, they all huddled together nervously trying to build up the courage to approach someone.

Adison spotted a very attractive man at the bar. Her colleagues urged her to walk by him and give him the SEE. Hesitantly, she began moving in his direction. As she got closer, her heart started racing. Her palms became sweaty, and she wondered what the hell she was doing. The guy turned his head and glanced at her, and out of instinct she looked away. She high-tailed it back to her friends and cried, "I can't do it!"

After that, the rest of the ladies were terrified as well.

The following week Adison told me her horror story. I told her that it was going to be hard to transition herself from being passive to assertive with men. She had trained herself to look away when a guy noticed her, so of course it would take some getting used to. She explained that she had been practicing with her coworkers, and they had gotten pretty good at the techniques. When she actually got to a bar and attempted to use them, however, she lost all confidence and couldn't do it. I told her that was to be expected because practicing with her girlfriends wasn't going to prepare her for the real thing. What she needed to do was practice in gamelike conditions.

Get in the Game

What exactly is a gamelike condition? Well, let's say you are a basketball player. Would it make sense to shoot hoops every day all by yourself? Probably not. When game time comes you wouldn't be able to make any shots because you wouldn't be used to someone trying to block you. So instead of practicing alone, it makes more sense to practice like you are in a game. Having someone try to block you while shooting hoops will help you ready yourself for what it will be like when it's time to really play. That's practicing in gamelike conditions.

Adison was not successful in the field because she was practicing with women she knew well and was comfortable with. The anxiety of prospecting comes from approaching someone you don't know. So how could she possibly get a true feel for it when she was rehearsing with Mary from Sales and Barb from Accounting?

I took Adison out that night. We didn't go to a bar. We didn't even go to a restaurant. We just walked the city streets. The downtown area was bustling and there were guys all around. I told her to just start smiling and making eye contact with any guy who walked by. Didn't matter how young, old, cute, or not so cute he was. The point was just to practice with men that she didn't know. We walked for blocks and blocks. Every time we passed a guy, she made up some excuse as to why she wasn't able to use the SEE Factor. Either the guy wasn't looking or he was looking too much. He was too far away or he was too close for comfort.

After walking around for an hour, we started our trek home. I told her that if she couldn't do it on the street with a guy she wasn't interested in, she would never be able to do it when she really needed to. Just then we passed a hole-in-the-wall bar with an outside patio. There was one waiter sitting at a table smoking a cigarette on his break. This was it, I told her. This was her very last chance. It was like watching a movie in slow motion. Adison took a deep breath and peeled her eyes off the ground. The guy exhaled a long and billowy cloud of smoke. She looked at him. He caught her eye. We had contact! Now all that had to happen was for Adison to smile an enthusiastic and confident smile. Could she do it? She had come this far, but I wasn't sure. A baby cried in the distance. It seemed like an eternity had passed. Then I saw it. The sides of her mouth began to curl. She was doing it. She was smiling! Upon seeing this, the waiter sat up in his chair, grinned from ear to ear and waved hello. Success! I turned to give Adison a pat on the back, but she was already around the corner, breathing into her doggy bag and trying to catch her breath.

When you have conditioned yourself to avoid other people's eye contact, then it will be a bit uncomfortable to use SEE . . . at first. But the more you practice in gamelike conditions, the easier it will become. Start out like Adison, smiling at people as you walk by them on the street. Practice on women if it helps you warm up. Do it whenever you are out of your house. It doesn't matter where you are or who you look at. No one shies away from a friendly smile. The more you practice, the easier it will be for you to do. Then when you spot that handsome man across the room, you won't hesitate for a second. You will know what to do and you will get what you want.

As for the other techniques in the book, you must apply the same advice. Don't wait for Mr. Perfect to come along and then start using the Mirror Theory. Practice it on a Mr. Okay-for-

Now or Mr. Nice-but-Not-Really-My-Type. Try using Sense of Urgency on your backup guy. You won't feel as much pressure if you practice with men you aren't seriously interested in; however, you will get a feel for how to use the techniques and how men will react to them. Then when it's really game time, you won't question yourself. You will be confident in everything you say and do.

Remember that your love life is within your control. You can make it happen. There are plenty of available men in the world just waiting to meet you. It's up to you, however, to provide them with the opportunity to do so. No more sitting around and complaining you don't have a boyfriend and will never get married. Get up and go after what you want. Pay careful attention to Buying Signs. If you aren't getting good ones, move on to the next. Keep your communication short and simple, and always end your dates at the Height of Impulse. Finally, hold back your Bullets until you know you have found the right relationship for yourself. Now that you have a road map to guide you, you won't get lost . . . and now you won't lose him. Your happy ending is out there waiting for you. Go after it.

Good luck and happy prospecting!

Also by Jess McCann

Was It Something I Said?
The Answer to All Your Dating Dilemmas

I t's not unusual for Jess McCann to receive a frantic late–night call from one of her clients asking for advice while out on a date. Now she tackles some of the trickiest and most troublesome scenarios in today's complicated dating world in her new indispensable dating survival guide, *Was It Something I Said? The Answers to All Your Dating Dilemmas*. With real–life situational questions that frequently come up in ·her date–coaching practice, Jess McCann gives play–by–play instructions for how to best respond to each scenario. So if you're not sure how to get him to stop texting and start calling, whether or not to friend him on Facebook, or if you should tell him you're dating other guys, this book has the answers. It will empower you to handle love's little challenges the right way—it's like having your own personal dating coach!

Index

alcohol, 46, 240–243, 250–251
    drunk dialing, 247–250
    on a first date, 244–247
    prospecting, 243–244
anticipation, 161–162
appearances, 50–52, 84–85
assumptions about men's
    feelings, 190–191

bars, 68–69, 81
begging (*see also*
    desperation), 20
being different, 56–61
blaming the guy, 2–3
blind dates, 108–111
body language, 141–144
    Mirror Theory, 144–146

breakup excuses, 216–218
breast implants, 46
Bullet Theory, 157–158
    anticipation, 162–163
    expiring, 163–164
    kissing, 163–164
    sex, 160–168
burning out, 121
buyer's remorse, 218–219,
    224–225
Buying Signs, 21–22, 98–99,
    267
    high to low interest,
        107–108, 231–232
    low interest, 100–104,
        106, 236
    upon meeting, 104–105

calling him, 18, 23, 25

Can't Buy Me Love, 151

career, 10–12

cheated on, 9

college dating, 7–8

Coming to America, 38

commitment

    men's phobia, 1–2, 21

    rushing, 169–170

complaining on a date,
    113–115

confidence, 45–49, 75

Crawford, Cindy, 60

date coaching, 13

desperation, 23, 237

diet, healthy, 46

divorce, 131, 183

doing too much, 181–183

    dangers of, 183–184

dressing right, 50–51,
    54–55, 58

    repeating outfits, 59

    revealing clothes, 55–56

drunk dialing (*see* alcohol)

dumped, 9

eHarmony, 53, 244

email, 115, 147, 217

emotional decisions, 24–25

ending at the height of
    impulse, 120–123

exclusivity, 89–91, 93–95

exercise, 47–49

eye contact, 73–74

Facebook, 71, 80, 92–94, 101

fear of loss, 192, 195–196, 232

    creating, 196–197

    losing it, 198–199, 200–201

    men's point of view, 193

    women's point of view,
        194

fear of rejection, 75

filling the funnel (*see*
    exclusivity)

friends

    dropping for a
        relationship, 8

game playing, 26–28, 31

    necessity of, 29

grocery stores, 70

hard to get, 72, 78–79, 135

Hilton, Paris, 146

hobbies, 41

Home Shopping Network,
    203

ice breakers, 76–80, 264
indifference, 126–128, 135–
    136
    early in relationship,
        136–140
    in sales, 132–133
insecurity, 45–46
interests, developing, 40–41
Internet dating, 22, 53, 66,
    70–71
intimidating men, 27

jealousy, 154
Jones Effect, 148–149
    defined, 151–152
    early in the relationship,
        152–153
    going overboard, 153–154

kissing on first date, 163–164
KISS principle, 22, 40, 108–
    109, 112–113, 125
    email and texting, 115–116

Liberty Tavern, 76
LinkedIn, 71

listening skills, 111–112,
    116–117
losing his interest, 229–232
    regaining interest, 233–234
    signs, 238–240
love
    falling, 140, 199–200
    saying "I love you," 19–20,
        24, 187–189

makeover, 50–51, 54–55,
    57–58
making the first move, 77–78
marathons, 69
marriage, 5–7, 13, 90, 168–
    170, 187, 193, 202
    failing, 225–227
    pressuring, 174, 191–192,
        207
    timetable, 207–209
    when men bring it up, 177
Match.com, 53, 117, 122, 245
Mirror Theory, 20, 141–142,
    234, 267
    explained, 144–146
    in non–date
        communication, 147–
        148
    voice, 146–147
Montag, Heidi, 60

narcissism, 86
neediness, 23, 128–131, 137

OKCupid, 53
Oktoberfest, 79
online profiles (*see also*
    Internet dating), 82, 87
opening up, 39–40
opinions, having, 38, 42–43
over–committing, 8, 28–29
overexposure, 120–121

people pleasing, 184–185
plastic surgery, 60
playing hard to get, 18
politics, 42
practicing your techniques,
    264–266
prejudging, 82–85, 87
priorities, 28–29
proposal, 5–7
prospecting, 64–66, 76
    alcohol, 243–244
    bars and clubs, 68–69
    good places for men, 68
    law of averages, 70–71
    switching your routine,
        69–70

qualifying men, 176–178

relationship hopping, 130–
    131
relationships
    building, 32
    "the talk," 91–92, 188
    timing, 140–141
rejection, 258–260
    handling it, 261–263
repeating relationship
    mistakes, 2
restaurant openings, 69, 102
Roberts, Nora, 67
Rules, The, 72
sales, 10–12, 14, 22–23, 56–
    57, 63–64, 84, 89, 121–122
    as part of life, 17–18
    closing, 155–157, 172–173,
        185–187
    desperation, 143
    fear of loss, 194–195
    filling the funnel, 89–90
    indifference, 133–134
    losing deals, 253–254
    loving the product,
        43–44, 49
    qualifying customers,
        175–176
    quality customers, 227

rejection, 258–259

sweetening the deal, 178–181

understanding the product, 35–37, 43–44

saying no (*see also* Silent No), 119–121

SEE factor, 72–75, 105, 263, 265

self–esteem, 44–45

self–respect, 163

Sense of Urgency, 203–204, 267

closing, 206–208

creating early, 204–206

sex, 16, 46, 107, 158–160, 164–167, 171

Sex and the City, 120

Silent No, 210–211

reasons, 214–216

recognizing, 212–214

sleeping over, 124–126

smiling, 73, 75

smoking, 45

Socrates, 41

spending too much time, 117–119

sports, 40

stalking, 22

stood up, 9

strategy, 30–31

Styker Medical, 209–210

sunglasses, 75

texting, 24–25, 97, 106, 115–116, 136, 147, 234, 248

therapy, 131

validating your behavior, 26

waiting for him to call, 252–254

when it works, 257–258

wine tastings, 69